East Meadow Public Library
1886 Front Street
East Meadow, NY 11554
(516) 794-2570
www.eastmeadow.info
APR 17 2017

D0812273

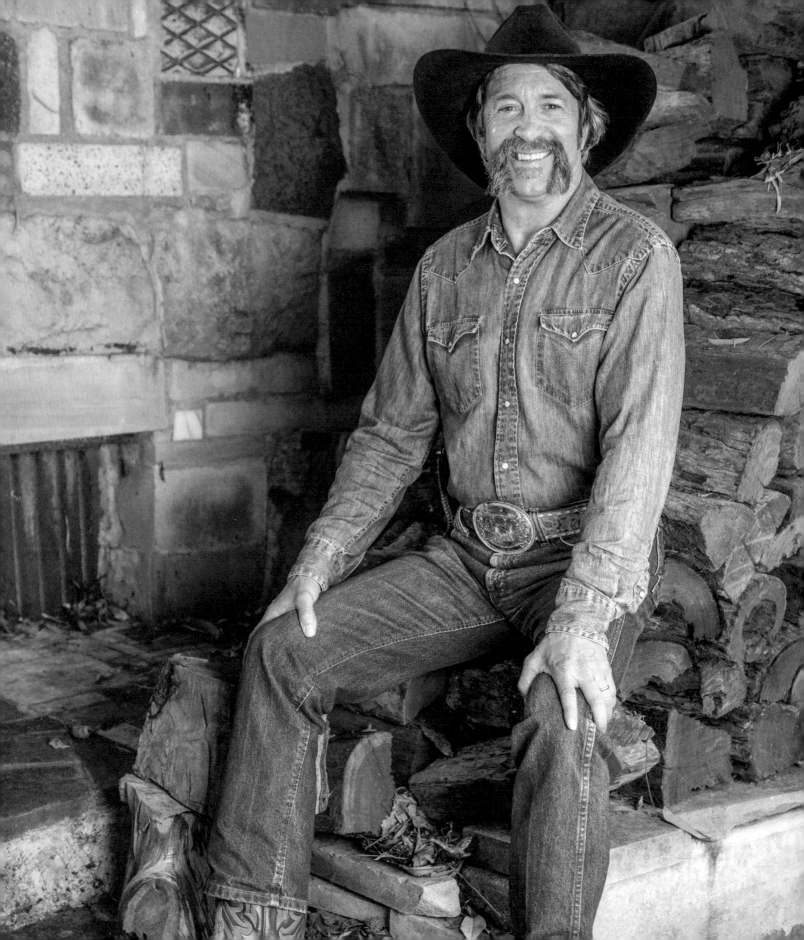

TEXAN BBQ

A SMOKIN' GOOD COOKBOOK

Robert Louis Murphy

NEW HOLLAND

I dedicate this book to my sister, Maxine.

Contents

INTRODUCTION

Cooking outdoors is just more fun than cooking indoors. Food prepared outdoors seems to taste better. Everyone seems to be in a better mood and there always seems to be a party atmosphere.

I can even remember making mud pies outside with my sister Maxine and thinking that they tasted, well ... sort of good. Being outside has an effect on your appetite and makes you hungry. It was because I was hungry that I decided to learn how to cook in the outdoors.

It all started when I was an energetic young boy in the woods with my rifle and a box of matches. At first, I first tried to catch, cook and eat a rabbit—it tasted horrible. I vowed to bring salt on my next hunt, then after that, some butter and a skillet. For me, the art of cooking with sticks grew from those humble beginnings. Eventually I found myself in the Rocky Mountains, elk hunting on horseback with a portable kitchen on fully-loaded pack mules. I once stayed in the mountains for so long that I had a mild culture shock when I came down and rejoined society.

As a youngster, I also began instructing welders about how to put together some custom barbecues. During the first half of my life I lived much closer to the land and knew full well what it was to take responsibility for my own food. It gave me a deep respect for what I was cooking, and a real understanding for the whole process of preparing good basic food. Sadly, I think most chefs today have skipped the first part of that process.

Before I was a teenager, I could take my hunting rifle and feed 50 people later that day. I have to wonder if some cooks could do that now. I was lucky to have been raised in a place where cooking outdoors is a way of life.

Texas is home to more barbecue places than anywhere in the world. There are steak houses where cooks have not only refined beef cooking but also have helped to develop the modern-day beef industry. Mexican food and cooking traditions have also influenced Texas probably more than any other place, and have likewise had a huge impact on my own cooking. Texas has an endless array of outdoor cooking apparatus (barbecue pits) and people there have refined these cooking methods to an art form.

I have a deep sense of pride for the Texan way of life that influences what and how I cook and I'm delighted to be able to share that. Nowadays men and women are doing more of their own cooking outdoors and searching for more unusual ways to use their cooking skills for cooking outside to create more enjoyable varieties of delicious meals.

This book has some tried and true recipes to help you if you are on that journey.

I have cooked most of the Tex-Mex dishes that I ever liked for my family and friends—some of them were not the best but some were great. Regrettably, if it was my recipe, I hardly ever bothered to write anything down, until now.

It's been a long journey from making mud pies with my sister.

When you're starting, keep it simple.

BUYING A BARBECUE

The barbecue is your best "non-human" friend. Whether buying a barbecue or building your own, think about your barbecue set up as a place where you'll have fun.

The best advice I can give you is get the best you can afford at the time. Shop around. Talk to lots of people. Learn the limitations and the strengths of both barbecues and barbecuers.

Since there are literally hundreds of different varieties of barbecues, you're best off getting whatever you can afford and whatever is available in your local area. At the very least, whether wood-fired, coal-fired, gas or even electric, a barbecue should have the following features.

Make sure your barbecue has a cooking surface where you can control both indirect heat (cooking away from the main source of heat) and direct heat (cooking near or on top of the main source of heat).

The barbecue should also have a warming rack where the meat can rest without getting cold.

If you can, get a smoker either attached to the barbecue or as a separate unit, as this will create a whole new world of possibilities for you.

Be Safe When Barbecuing

It's important that you set up your barbecue so that you have happy, pleasant experiences cooking outdoors. Set up your barbecue set up in a safe place—level, partially °shaded, not crowded—and check that everything is working properly. Make sure it is in a ventilated area and ensure you have a garden hose nearby or have a fire extinguisher at hand.

It is pretty easy for someone to get their barbecue too close to their house and wind up burning down the house. It has happened so keep your barbecue and combustible materials away from buildings.

Some of the worst food I have ever had at barbecues was cooked by someone cooking with too much wine (not in the food). It is wise to have a designated (sober) cook.

Watch out for the kids. Have some safety rules worked out with your children and keep the dogs and cats out of the fire.

It's also important that you do not leave an open grill unattended.

Keep your barbecue clean. This will ensure that your barbecued food tastes the way you want it to.

Lastly, ensure you comply with fire restrictions. The fire trucks come to my place sometimes, but it is not during fire danger alerts—I think they are just hungry.

Left to right: Michael, Robert and Maxine Murphy.

Glyn Ed Murphy

THE ART OF OUTDOOR COOKING

Barbecue traditionally meant cooking with wood on a low heat and smoking your meat. Now the definition can mean any kind of cooking outdoors. I like to think that a basic contemporary definition is just cooking outside with wood, charcoal or gas.

Cooking Equipment and Techniques

No matter what you are cooking you have to manage the heat—you have to regulate it. This can only come through experience and practice. You get experience from making mistakes. I have a lot of experience.

My father used to say, "if you can play golf it doesn't matter about the clubs. You can play with a grubbing hoe, or if you can shoot pool you can play with a broom handle."

I say, "if you can cook, you can cook on a hubcap." With this in mind, I recommend that you start with any equipment that suits you and your budget. You can always progress as your skill level, opportunities, dedication and enthusiasm increases. As a basic requirement, a campfire is all you need. In Texas I cooked on, designed, built and bought some Cadillac (the very best) barbecues. These could cook up a huge meal for a bunch of hungry people.

Since then I've built 'barbecues' in any old place you can burn leaves. Sometimes, I have found a grill, cleaned it, and started cooking with sticks. That suited me fine. I've gone from one primitive fire grill to another and even then I've cooked some pretty good stuff. I eventually bought the cheapest gas-fired grill I could find and then only because my wife insisted. Now I have a really good barbecue that's just wonderful, but I still enjoy cooking on the ground sometimes. In terms of basic equipment, you need:

- » steel cooking grill
- » a good cast-iron skillet or some kind of frypan that can take an open flame and hot coal punishment
- » barbecue fork and tongs
- » oven mitts (personally, I use leather gloves)
- » an internal meat temperature gauge
- » sharp knives.

Knives

I recommend that you get the best knives you can afford from a reputable, specialist knife store.

Keeping your knives in good condition is not hard to do. Just clean them and hone them with a steel each time you use them. Hand wash after use: it is best not to put your kitchen knives in a dishwasher. Keep each knife in a sheath; leather or plastic or just have something to cover the blade. This protects the blade and you.

Get your friendly knife store person to show you how to use a steel and "Bob's your uncle" as the expression goes, or if you're my niece or nephew call me Robert. At the very least, you will need:

- » chef's knife
- » boning knife
- » utility knife
- » paring knife
- » knife sharpener—something that works well like a diamond whetstone, whet rock or steel.

GET THE BEST CUTS

Choose the right cut for the right dish. The barbecue is the perfect instrument for low and slow cooking.

The amount of marbling (intra-muscular fat) in beef affects cooking times and techniques.

Some cuts need to be tenderized (like flank steak or round steak). Get your butcher to do it or learn how to do it yourself. For some brief instructions, see 'How to tenderize meat' on page 18.

Beef

The top cuts for steak:

» Tenderloin, also known as filet steak, is the most tender cut of beef (as its name implies).
» Rib-eye, also known as the scotch filet, is the tender cut that sits around the ribs. It is the cut that steak-lovers love most. When cooked correctly, it is full of flavor.
» T-bone consists of both top loin (strip) and tenderloin steaks, connected by a tell-tale T-shaped bone.

The top beef cuts for slow cooking

» Brisket
» Shin (Gravy) Beef (Shank)
» Chuck Steak
» Blade Steak (from the chuck section)
» Round Steak
» Topside Steak (from the round section)

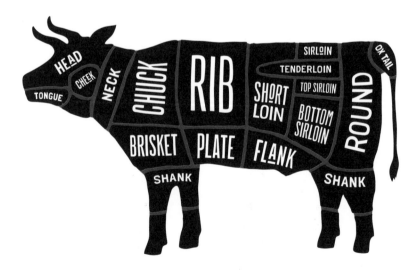

Lamb

The top lamb cuts for slow cooking
- » Leg Roasts
- » Boneless Shoulder
- » Boneless Forequarter (the breast section)
- » Shanks
- » Neck Chops

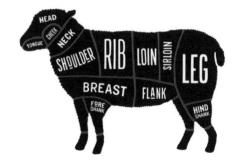

Pork

The top pork cuts for slow cooking
- » Pork Shoulder (Boston butt)
- » Forequarter Chops (from Picnic Ham section)
- » Pork Neck
- » Ribs
- » Ham Hock
- » Bone-in Roasts

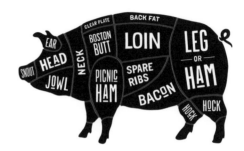

Chicken

The top chicken cuts for slow cooking
- » Whole Chicken
- » Thigh Pieces
- » Drumsticks
- » Maryland (combination of Drumstick and Thigh)

GET THE BEST RESULTS

Knowing how to cut, tenderize, store, and cook your cuts of meat is paramount if you want a great result for barbecued meats. Many of my recipes talk about the internal temperature of meats as they are cooking. A guide for internal temperatures is included here so that you can achieve either the perfect rare, medium rare and medium barbecued steak.

How To Cut Meat

When cutting meat, my advice is this: *Make your butcher your best friend.*

Get him or her to cut the meat according to the instructions I'll give you in the recipes in this book.

In terms of cookery, the general rule is to cut against the muscle grain and to remove all excess sinew and gristle that you wouldn't want to eat anyway. Like everything else, this takes practice, but if your butcher is your best friend, you can ask for pointers (preferably during times when things are a bit slow in the shop). Your often get the chance to watch butchers as they cut your meat anyway. Just pay attention and don't be shy about asking questions. True professionals love sharing their expertise with interested amateurs. They're actually flattered that you're taking an interest.

How To Tenderize Meat

Sometimes meat needs to be tenderized to make it easier to cook and eat. Either get your butcher to do it or do the following.

Put a moist tea towel on your kitchen counter or table. Place a chopping board on top of the towel. The towel will stop the board from slipping.

Place the meat you need to tenderize between two layers of cling wrap on the chopping board.

Take a meat tenderizing mallet and hit the meat with the textured side of the mallet.

Make sure you don't strike the meat straight down. Strike it at a slight angle, with either a pushing or pulling motion, while still managing to hit the meat with the flat surface of the mallet. Keep hitting the meat until you have covered the surface on both sides and it is all relatively the same thickness.

Practice this with small cuts of meat at first. You can later progress to larger cuts. Most of the time you're only tenderizing flank or round steak, both of which are relatively thin.

In the end it might still be easier for the butcher to do this for you, as he already has a specially-dedicated machine to tenderize your meat that can be done in about 15 seconds. But you have to ask.

How To Store Meat

Barbecuing, especially smoking, actually started as a method to preserve meat for long periods of time. Done properly, barbecued smoked meat is predisposed to keep. But, thanks to the marvels of modern refrigeration, storing meat has never been easier. So now you can have the best of both worlds.

Fresh Meat Storage Tips

» Make sure your meat is sealed properly. Don't buy it if it is smells off or is discolored.
» Buy your meat as fresh as you can, preferably on the same day that it's delivered to your butcher. Just ask.
» Make sure that when you do store meat in the refrigerator, that the meat is well wrapped and kept away from other foods, preferably in its own meat drawer. Always keep it cold.

GOOD ADVICE FROM foodsafety.gov

Bacon is safe to eat for up to a week in the refrigerator—but raw sausage should be eaten within two days. Both can be frozen for a month, and some sausage will freeze for twice as long.

Ground meats (beef, veal, pork, or poultry) can be refrigerated for one to two days and frozen for three to four months.

Hot dogs will last two weeks in the refrigerator unopened and should be eaten within three to five days of opening (hot dogs can go a couple of days longer). In the freezer, they'll last one to two months.

Raw poultry lasts just a day or two in the refrigerator (at a temperature of 40°F (or colder), but up to a year in the freezer. Cooked poultry can be refrigerated a few days longer and should be frozen no longer than 2 to 6 months.

Red meat and pork can remain in the refrigerator up to five days and can be frozen for four months to one year. Leftover cooked meat will last three to four days in the refrigerator and two to six months in the freezer.

How To Cook Meat

Cooking meat is, I'll admit, an art and like any art, what constitutes a perfectly cooked piece of meat is subjective. However, here are some ideas about cooking that will give you great results.

Use an internal meat thermometer to get just the right temperature, as recommended in my recipes. Using a thermometer takes the guess work out of cooking. Even though I have had decades of experience, I still use one.

Do not overcook meat unless you enjoy eating it that way. For me, overcooked meat is dry and tough. Ideally, meat should be pink inside, even if ever so slightly. But if you do like meat well done, or if you accidentally overcook meat, you can always hide a multitude of sins with a good sauce. There are plenty of sauce recipes in this book to try.

Don't cook with too much or too little heat. You'll see my suggestions for the right degree of heat in each recipe.

Make sure the coals (if using) have died down before cooking. If the fire is flaring or the charcoal is red hot, it will end up burnt on the outside and raw in the middle. Heat control is the secret to any good cooking.

Preheat your grill. The grill needs to be hot enough so that you get those attractive grill marks.

Reverse Sear Cooking Method

A reverse sear involves cooking on a low, indirect heat until the meat reaches an internal temperature for rare, medium rare or medium then cooking on a direct heat for a couple of minutes longer before resting the meat.

The following table, "Heat guide for an internal meat thermometer", shows the recommended temperatures for reverse sear cooking.

Heat guide for an internal meat thermometer. Take meat off the bbq once it reaches the desired internal temperature and then place on direct heat to reach the target temperature. Turn once or twice whilst on direct heat. It will only take 2-3 minutes on each side to be cooked perfectly.

BEEF	Internal Temperature	Target Temperature
Rare	110°–115°F (43°–46°C)	120°–125°F (49°–51°C)
Medium rare	135°F (50°C)	145°–155°F (60°–69°C)
Medium	150°F (60°C)	160°F (70°C)
LAMB	Internal Temperature of Lamb	Target Temperature
Medium rare	120°–125°F (45°–47°C)	130°–135°F (55°–57°C)
Medium	135°F (60°C)	145°F (67°C)

How To Rest And Serve Meat

Resting is a period of time, after cooking, when the meat is no longer on direct heat. After cooking your meat, rest it in a warm place such as on the warming rack of your barbecue.

Meat is a little like a sponge full of water. When you cook it, the sponge dehydrates a little as water leaves the meat cells. Resting your meat is an essential part of the cooking process and one that people too often ignore.

When meat is allowed to rest (away from the heat) after cooking, the juice of the meat is redistributed. This gives the meat enough time to rehydrate, making it tender and full of flavor. This results in a more tender and juicer piece of meat when you cut it.

Rest meat on a wire rack in a warm place. For fried foods, rest on a wire rack then pat after with a paper towel to keep it crispy and to drain off the excess oil. Avoid leaving fried food resting directly on paper as this can make the food start to sweat and it may be soggy.

The time of rest depends on the size of the meat portion. The general rule is one minute for every 3½ oz (100 g) of meat. Serve the food as soon as possible after the required resting time has been allowed to take place.

If you're really dedicated, spend some time learning about the art of presentation—we eat with our eyes, as much as with our mouths.

How To Smoke Brisket

There are many methods for cooking brisket in an oven or on small barbecues, but to smoke a big cut of brisket properly would be hard on a small barbecue. This way of preparing brisket was first cooked in Texas. Several groups are claiming responsibility—cowboys, German migrants and African Americans. It doesn't really matter who first cooked it—what's important, is that this is truly worth the effort.

This was a rough cut of meat that was not preferred and was given to the ranch hands who learned how to cook it low, slow and tender. Texans also developed the modern-day steel barbecue pits built out of huge pieces of pipe that were left on ranches from ruined oil wells—a relict of the Texan oil booms that took place in the early 1900s. I was cooking on these and designing my own before I was a teenager.

To cook a good smoked brisket, you need an offset smoker, which allows you to keep the temperature low and steady for long periods of time. You have to have good wood such as hickory, oak, mesquite (ironbark will work a bit) or any of the fruitwoods. Pecan is my absolute favorite.

Ideally, the brisket should be from a really big cut of meat from a 500–600 lbs (240–280 kg) carcass. I like to cook just the point of the brisket (which in this case would weigh around 11–14 lbs (5–6 kg) because the flat of the brisket is too thin and cannot withstand 10 hours (or more) of cooking. I have cooked briskets for over 20 hours to get them perfect.

You can cook a smaller brisket in less time, and it does not have to be smoked. This is just the best way I know of to cook a large brisket. Even though it looks like a meteorite when it comes out it is as tender as it should be. You can roughly estimate when a brisket will be done by allowing 45 to 75 minutes per 1 lb (500 g) when cooking at 145° F (72° C). It will be cooked when the internal temperature reaches 190° F (88° C). Rest and cut when the internal temperature reaches 145° F (72° C) for best results.

How To Work Out Serving Portions

When meat is the main part of your meal, a serving for one person should generally be about the size of your palm or about 3 oz (90 g). This is considered a healthy portion of protein for a meal. For larger appetites, you may want to allow 6–8 oz (about 175–250 g). If the meat is only a part of a recipe or a serving, such as say a pasta dish, allow smaller portions per person. This should help you calculate how much to buy for how many people.

That's all for my tips on getting the best from your barbecue. Now let's get cooking.

COOKING TIPS

Knowing some tricks of the trade can make the difference between a great meal and a not-so-great one. Use the following tips to get the best results from your barbecue cooking, They are listed in order of the chapters and recipes in this book. First comes beef. Lamb and pork follow in the next chapter. Chicken is followed by side dishes and so on.

Tips on cooking beef steak

Firstly, a bit about beef. Aged beef is not that expensive when you stop to think that meat that is not aged has a lot of moisture content, so you are paying for water. Thick steaks with a high fat content or more marbling generally must be cooked at a higher heat (direct) initially and sometimes placed in a low heart (indirect) to render the fat inside. Your internal meat temperature thermometer will help you get it just right.

» Grill the steaks 4–5 inches (10–12 cm) from a medium direct heat 10–12 minutes for medium, turning once halfway through the grilling process.
» Cooking time will always depend on the thickness of your steaks, what type of barbecue you are cooking on and how hot your fire is, so get yourself some experience cooking in a variety of places with different cuts of different thickness.

Tips For Cooking a Lamb Leg or Shoulder

» Leave the bone in for flavor, even though it will be harder to carve.
» Use a dry rub rather than a marinade as lamb is already tender.
» Cook in a stock and baste a few times.
» A good roasting temperature is 320ºF (160ºC).
» Have an internal meat thermometer handy and use it.
» Rest the lamb after it has cooked and carve it against the grain.

Tips on cooking pork

In the recipes there are very specific guidelines for cooking different cuts, because different cuts need different temperatures, so take care to use those specific temperature guides.

» Keep it simple. Some of the best barbecue places in the world have surprisingly simple methods and recipes without elaborate marinades or seasonings. Make it easy on yourself.
» Some of the best barbecue sauces came from those who used the cheapest ingredients because they had very little money.
» If you have a really good cut of pork, you don't have to have a fancy marinade—just some simple spices that you like will do fine.
» Use sauces, marinades and rubs only when you think it's appropriate. You'll find some recipes for making sauces, marinades and rubs in this book.
» Pork cooks much better with the skin dry which helps to make great crackling.

Tips on Cooking Large Cuts of Pork

»   Before you start cooking, the meat needs to start at room temperature, be dry, then be oiled and seasoned.
»   If you intend to cook a large piece of pork for a long period of time, allow 25 minutes per pound (500 g) at 400° F (200°C) then it might take a while for it to reach room temperature. If this is the case, wrap the meat to prevent surface evaporation, which will dry it out.
»   Preheat your barbecue or oven and try to maintain an even, steady temperature.

Tips on Cooking Chicken

No matter what kind of barbecue you have, you need to have two cooking zones for direct and indirect heating.

»   Anything you cook that takes more than an hour needs to be sealed or wrapped to keep it tender, juicy and moist and to keep those flavors from escaping.
»   For a whole chicken, half chicken or even large pieces, these all need to be cooked on indirect heat. For half chickens or large individual pieces, use toothpicks to hold the skin in place and stop the skin from shrinking.
»   Cook chicken low and slow.
»   The bone in chicken doubles the cooking times. Breast and thighs cook differently. The breast is done when it reaches an internal temperature of 165°F (72°C). The thigh is done when it reaches 185°F (83°C). Use an internal meat thermometer to get the best results.
»   And you need to rest to be at your best too. The juices try to get away from the heat. Always let your meat sit for 2–5 minutes after cooking. The larger the cut, the more rest time it needs.

Tips on Cooking Side Dishes

Side dishes can be heroes too. At least give 'em a chance.

»   Work out what side dish to cook by looking at your main. If you have a heavy main dish, make a light side dish and get a balanced meal this way.
»   Try to cook what is fresh, seasonal or at its peak.
»   If the dinner is looking sparse, make a fresh salad, or include a salsa (pages 169–172).

Tips on Preparing Sauces

»   Match your sauce to go with what you're cooking. This is often a matter of taste, so make sure the sauce you use goes with your meal and actually makes it better.
»   Gather your ingredients and tools first. Read your sauce recipe before you need to prepare your meal and make sure you have what you need to make it.
»   Get the best fresh ingredients you can and taste them to make sure that they're OK.
»   Figure out when you can make the sauce—the day before, a couple of hours in advance or before you serve.
»   Thicken most sauces by reducing them, or use corn flour instead of flour because the consistency is better, but if you're gluten intolerant, use pure corn *starch*.
»   Don't forget to salt the sauce—but not too much.

» Don't forget to taste the sauce. For some reason, it is always easy for me to forget this one and it has happened to me more than a few times. Check and taste before you serve.

Tips on Preparing Marinades

» Marinade flavor is mostly on the outside, so it's a surface treatment. For big cuts of beef and chicken marinating is necessary because these meats are so dense and the salt in the marinade penetrates the meat to make it more tender. That's why marinades should always have salt. More porous foods like eggplant can absorb more flavor, so they don't need a marinade.
» Marinades work especially well (they'll work faster and more flavor goes in) on thinner cuts of meat that have been tenderized. Marinades also keep foods from drying out during the cooking process. The oil seals in the juices and the sugar in marinade helps the meat to brown quickly.
» It does not take long (15 minutes–1 hour) to marinate seafood and most vegetables.
» Do not marinate in aluminum, copper or cast iron as the acid in the marinade will react unpleasantly with these metals. Use a plastic, glass or ceramic container instead.
» Small lamb cuts need no more than 30 minutes of marinating, covered in the refrigerator.
» Chicken, turkey, and pork need a minimum of 2 to 3 hours, but 6 to 8 hours is best. The skin on chicken or turkey does not allow marinades to penetrate, so feel free to skin your birds.
» Most large cuts of beef (but not steaks) need to marinate for 6 to 24 hours.
» Steaks generally don't need a marinade if they are from really good beef.

Tips on Preparing Rubs

» Rubs are mixtures of herbs and spices used to pre-season meat before cooking.
» Rubs classically include salt, sugar and condiments. The aim of the flavor elements is to create a balance of flavors—salty, sweet, sour and bitter. The purpose of a rub is to bring out the best in the flavor of the meat.
» A rub also makes a crust on the cooked meat, which adds a further element, texture.
» The sugar in a rub will caramelize, so that the meat retains its flavor while adding a good color too. So put your rub together, sprinkle it on, and rub it in.

10 Steps For Successful Barbecuing

Clean your grill before your start. Always get your barbecue going before you cook and start with proper heat temperature.

1. Take an onion, cut it in half and go over the grill grates with it while the grill is heating. Remember food hygiene. Keep things clean. Wear gloves and use barbecue tools. Don't use your hands.
2. Before you start cooking, oil the flat plate or grill.
3. Allow meats to come to room temperature before cooking. Don't cook cold meat! Wait until it reaches room temperature first.
4. Create heat zones, an indirect (cooler) zone and a direct heat (hotter) zone.
5. Give the things you are cooking some space on the barbecue. Do not overcrowd your grill.
6. Make use of aluminum or tin foil. It's very versatile and can make cleanup very easy because you can just throw the foil away, so place it on working surfaces or in place of preparation plates and your cleanups will go a lot faster.
7. Heat your grill properly to make grill marks on the food that make you look like a pro.
8. Use a timer, with an alarm, so that you can stay on top of how long meat is cooking. This is especially important during long and slow cooking. Fortunately, most smart phones nowadays have easy-to-use timers.
9. When you finish grilling, clean the grill with a wire brush while the grill is still warm. Don't wait, it only takes a few seconds and you can do this while your meat is resting.
10. And don't forget to rest meat after cooking.

Chapter 1

BEEF

BARBECUED HAMBURGER

Serves 4

* *

For barbecued hamburger you need ground beef (mince). It's best to get this from your butcher and get them to make you a medium grind of chuck steak that's the right proportion of meat to fat—75% meat to 25% fat. Now this might seem like a lot of fat but, if you don't have the right ratio of meat to fat, you wind up with crumbled hamburger because the patty won't stick together. In any case, the excess fat will cook out, so don't worry.

INGREDIENTS

2 jalapeño peppers, chopped

2 medium white onions, diced

2 tablespoons extra virgin olive oil

16 oz (500 g) 100% ground beef

1 tablespoon Worcestershire sauce

salt and black pepper, to taste

extra virgin olive oil, for cooking

3 Kransky sausages (or other spiced sausage)

4 hamburger buns

4 slices cheddar cheese

4 cos lettuce leaves

1 red onion, sliced thinly

2 tomatoes, sliced thinly

2 dill pickles, sliced thinly

METHOD

» Set up grill to a medium high heat, 400°F (200°C).

» To make hamburger patties, add jalapeño peppers and white onions to a frypan with 2 tablespoons olive oil and sauté over medium heat, stirring until translucent in 2 tablespoons of oil, then set aside in a mixing bowl. Add the hamburger mince, Worcestershire sauce, salt and pepper.

» Form into 4 patties leaving an indent in the middle of each burger (the burgers will rise in the middle while cooking).

» Coat with patties with extra virgin olive oil before placing on an oiled barbecue grill. You'll know the temperature is right if the meat sizzles immediately upon contact. Cook patties to your liking, but I suggest that if you cook the patties past medium they will taste dry.

» Once cooked, remove from heat and allow at least 5–7 minutes after cooking for the burgers to rest.

» While patties are resting, grill the Kransky sausages and cut them into thin strips. Lightly brown the buns on the grill and place a cheese slice on the hot bun so that the cheese melts.

» Assemble burgers to your liking, stacking the bun with a cos lettuce leaf, red onion, tomato, dill pickle and the condiment of your choice.

NOTE Barbecue sauce, ketchup, mayonnaise or mustard all go well with burgers. Be creative with your cheeses. Any cheese that melts easily will do fine. Blue cheese is great but you don't need very much because it has such a strong flavor, especially when heated.

* *

FILET MIGNON STRIPS

Serves 4

* *

Traditionally done with the filet mignon cut, this recipe lends itself to any low-fat meat. It is essential that the bacon be thin cut due to fast cooking. You'll need 12 wooden toothpicks for this recipe.

INGREDIENTS

16 oz (450 g) filet mignon or lean steak
1 batch Beef Filet Marinade (page 177)
8 oz (250 g) streaky bacon, cut thinly

extra virgin olive oil, for cooking
Murphy's Ranch Dressing (page 173), optional

METHOD

» Preheat grill to medium high heat, 400ºF (200ºC).
» To make the steak strips, cut into 4 small steaks (the same size) and then cut each into thirds, so that they make 12 small strips. Place steak strips into a sealable plastic bag with the marinade and leave in the refrigerator for at least 4 hours or up to 2 days.
» Cut bacon into 12 strips about 4 inch (10 cm) long.
» When the strips have marinated, wrap a bacon strip around each steak strip and secure with a toothpick. The toothpick will double as the serving handle when the steak is cooked.
» Place the wrapped strips evenly on the oiled barbecue grill so that they don't touch.
» Cook until bacon is crispy, about 4–6 minutes, turning at least once to make sure bacon is crispy on all sides. Serve hot with Murphy's Ranch Dressing if desired.

NOTE Lean steak can include sirloin with the fat trimmed off. This recipe also works with any kind of venison because it is a lean meat. Substitute prosciutto or pancetta for the bacon if you wish.

* *

BONELESS RIB-EYE STEAK

Serves 4

* *

This is one of *the* traditional Texan recipes when barbecuing. These are the steaks to cook if you have to cook a lot or if you want to cook them perfectly. If I have to feed 30 or 40 people at a time, I'll tell them that I'm cooking rib-eye. It is easier to cook in large quantities because there is no bone to affect the rate of the steaks cooking, so they all cook evenly at the same time.

INGREDIENTS

4 boneless rib-eye steaks, each 12 oz (375 g), 1½ inch (3 cm) thick

extra virgin olive oil, for cooking
salt and pepper

METHOD

» Preheat your barbecue grill to high heat, 450ºF (230ºC).
» Rub the steaks with the oil and lightly season with salt and pepper. Lay on a tray in a single layer, cover with foil and allow the steaks to stay at room temperature for about 20–30 minutes.
» Use direct heat and cook for 5–8 minutes on each side depending on how well you like your meat cooked. Finish off on indirect heat to get the desired internal temperature. Allow to rest for 7–10 minutes before serving.

NOTE As a variation, try the Prime Rib Rub (page 188) or a marinade of your choice (pages 177–182. Also reverse searing works well on thick steaks. Nothing looks better than serving a perfectly-cooked steak on a bed of mashed potato—but if you don't let the steaks rest first, they're going to bleed all over your mash and look awful. So rest your steak before serving.

* *

SHISH KEBAB

Serves 4

* *

This is always popular at barbecues because you don't even need a plate to eat them. Although this recipe serves four, in reality, you can just multiply the ingredients to serve however many people you want and allow extra kebabs per person if you wish.

INGREDIENTS

16 oz (500 g) sirloin steak, trimmed of fat and cut into
  1½ inch (3 cm) cubes
1 batch Sirloin Marinade (page 178)
1 red bell pepper (capsicum)
1 green bell pepper (capsicum)
1 yellow bell pepper (capsicum)

1 corn cob
1 large red or white onion
16 small button mushrooms
extra virgin olive oil, for cooking
barbecue sauce (optional), to serve
ketchup (optional), to serve

METHOD

» Soak 4 stainless steel skewers or bamboo skewers in water for 15 minutes.
» Cut the steak into 1½ inch (3 cm) squares. Place in a plastic container or a large sealable plastic bag with the sirloin marinade. Reserve some marinade for basting while cooking. Place in the refrigerator for 3 hours or up to 2 days. Remove steak and discard excess marinade.
» Preheat barbecue grill to high heat, 450°F (230°C).
» Cut the bell peppers and onion into 1½ inch (3 cm) squares and corn into 1½ inch (3 cm) pieces.
» Thread a beef cube, one each of the bell peppers, onion and a mushroom alternately on the skewers. Repeat. Each skewer should hold about four cubes of steak along with their accompanying vegetables.
» Oil the surface of the barbecue grill and cook the kebabs until medium rare, turning and basting as needed with the reserved marinade.
» Serve hot on the skewers with any sauces of choice.

NOTE Consider a seafood option using shrimp (prawns) or lobster (cut in chunks) or make a 'surf and turf' by mixing the seafood with the steak. I have wrapped some pieces of chicken thighs with prosciutto and it was killer good. If using seafood, baste with garlic butter or a little oil so that the seafood cooks at the same rate as the vegetables. Make sure all the ingredients you put on the skewers are the same thickness and density so that they cook at the same rate. Although you can cook this on a gas barbecue, you really get the best results if you use charcoal. When turning the kebabs, use tongs or you'll end up burning yourself.

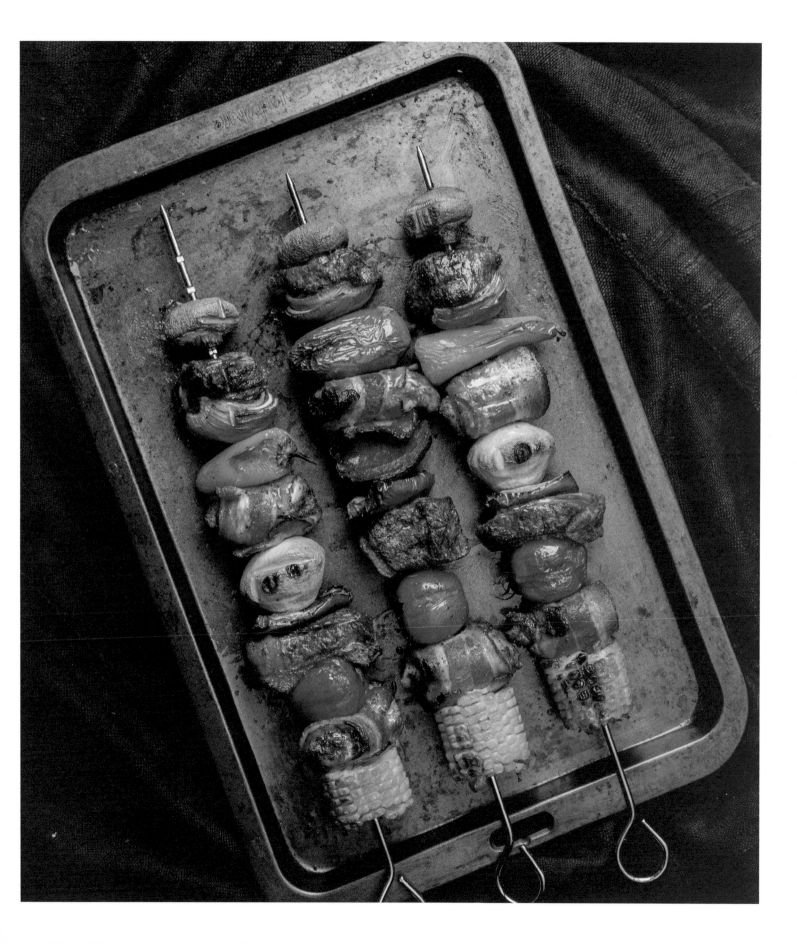

PATTY MELT

Serves 4

* *

Basically, this is fried hamburgers on rye bread instead of hamburger buns. The rye bread creates a really different flavor.

INGREDIENTS

8 tablespoons butter
1 large onion, cut in half, sliced thinly
16 oz (500 g) hamburger mince
3–4 tablespoons extra virgin oil, for cooking
8 slices rye bread, thick-sliced

4 slices cheddar cheese, or any cheese that melts
salt and freshly ground black pepper
4 slices Swiss cheese, torn into large pieces
½ pint (250 ml) water

METHOD

» Add butter to a frypan and sauté onion until nicely brown and caramelized to your taste. Set aside but keep warm.
» Preheat barbecue plate to a medium high heat, 400˚F (200˚C).
» Form the hamburger mince into 4 oval-shaped 4 oz (125 g) patties, roughly the same size and shape of your slices of rye bread.
» Coat patties with extra virgin olive oil (about ½ tablespoon) before placing on an oiled barbecue (1½ tablespoons oil).
» Grill your patties until they're done to your liking. Remember to put a dent in the middle of the patties because when they cook, the middle rises. Set aside for at least 5 minutes to rest.
» While the patties are resting, lightly fry the rye bread slices on one side on an oiled barbecue plate until golden brown.
» Remove from the plate, add a little more olive oil, and very lightly fry the other side.
» When done, place the slices (with the more-cooked side up) on a platter.
» On each of the slices, place a slice of cheddar, then a patty. Season the patty with salt and pepper to taste.
» Add a slice of Swiss cheese to each patty then the onion. Place the other slice of bread on top, with the lightly fried side up.
» Now fry the entire sandwiches on both sides in a frypan with some olive oil until they are golden brown, about 3–4 minutes.
» Cut each melt in half and serve straight away.

NOTE You could add a layer of fried bacon between the first cheese layer and the patty layer if desired. One side of the bread is deliberately under fried to keep the bread firm. When you do the final frying, you're cooking on the under-cooked side of the bread slices so that those surfaces don't burn—it's all in the detail.

* *

STEAK FINGERS

Serves 4

* *

Steaks don't really have fingers, any more than chickens or fish do, but this is a variation of fried steak that's sure to be popular. I can guarantee that, when you serve this up at a party or gathering, these will be the first to go.

INGREDIENTS

32 oz (1 kg) round or flank steak, tenderized
8 fl oz (250 ml) milk
2 medium eggs
8 oz (250 g) all-purpose (plain) flour
1 teaspoon salt

½ teaspoon black pepper
¼ teaspoon cayenne pepper
2 tablespoons butter, for frying
6 tablespoons extra virgin olive oil, for frying
Texan White Gravy (page 172), to serve

METHOD

» For the steak fingers, cut the steak into 1 inch (3 cm) strips against the grain of the meat and, however long or wide the steak is. Trim the fat as you go.
» Combine or whisk the milk and eggs in a separate bowl.
» Combine the flour, salt and spices in a plastic container with a lid or a zip-lock plastic bag and shake to mix thoroughly. Place the flour mixture on a shallow, wide plate.
» Dip the meat strips in the milk and egg mixture then dredge in the flour mix to coat all sides. Continue until the first 6 or 7 pieces are coated. This is about as many as you can cook at one a time.
» Heat the butter and oil in a large, cast-iron frypan (skillet) on the barbecue or stove top.
» Cook the first batch over a direct heat on your barbecue or in an oven on a medium high heat, 400°F (200°C). Remove when golden brown. This should take about 4–5 minutes at this temperature.
» While the batch of fingers is cooking, coat your next batch.
» When cooked, place the fingers on a wire rack to drain. Season with salt and pepper while still warm.
» Continue to fry the fingers 6 or 7 at a time depending on the size of your frypan or skillet.
» Serve with Texan White Gravy (page 172).

* *

TEXAN HOT DOGS

Serves 6

· ·

Did you know that Americans consume an average of 150 million hot dogs a day? Hot dogs were first invented in 1484 in Frankfurt, Germany, which is where we get the term, frankfurters. It's a truly international treat. In Norway, they keep their hot dogs simple, served with ketchup or mustard. But Brazilians generally pack more onto a hot dog than seems physically possible—with notable ingredients such as shoestring potato fries. Other toppings (most often depending on where you are) can include quail eggs, mashed potatoes, corn, peas, cheese and marinara sauce.

INGREDIENTS

1 tablespoon extra virgin olive oil
1 large brown onion, chopped
12 slices streaky bacon
6 all-beef hot dogs or Kransky sausages
hot dog buns, toasted
green relish or corn relish, to taste

3 medium tomatoes, sliced thinly
lettuce leaves, shredded
yellow or American mustard, to serve
ketchup, to serve
chutney, to serve

METHOD

» Heat barbecue to medium temperature. On barbecue plate or in a frypan on the barbecue, add the onion and cook until soft. If they brown a little, that is fine. Remove and set aside.
» Turn up the heat to medium high and add the bacon. Cook until crisp. Remove and place on paper towels to drain excess oil.
» Cook beef hot dogs or Kranskys on the barbecue grill, turning to make sure they are brown on all sides.
» On each bun place onion, 2 rashers bacon, hot dog/Kransky, relish, tomatoes and lettuce. Top with mustard, ketchup and chutney and serve.

NOTE You can heat up some chili and have a chili dog or melt some cheese for a chili cheese dog. You can make these without bacon, with Pico de Gallo (page 127), or use any sausage you prefer. Coleslaw is another popular addition as is sauerkraut.

SMOKED BEEF TENDERLOIN

Serves 10-12

• •

A traditional Texan recipe, you can use various spice rubs for tenderloin. For best results, apply to tenderloin a couple of days before you cook and serve it. You'll need some fruit wood for smoking for this recipe.

INGREDIENTS

1 beef tenderloin about 4–5 lb (2–2½ kg), trimmed
1–2 tablespoons extra virgin olive oil

salt and freshly ground black pepper, to taste
olive oil cooking spray

METHOD

» Preheat barbecue (with lid down) to 250º–300ºF (120º–140ºC).
» Remove meat from the refrigerator and let stand at room temperature for 20–30 minutes.
» Pat meat dry and brush with extra virgin olive oil and season with salt and pepper.
» Place tenderloin on the cooking surface on indirect heat.
» Smoke the tenderloin, maintaining temperature inside the smoker at 275º–300˚F (130º–140ºC), on indirect heat for 45 minutes or until a meat thermometer inserted in thickest portion of the tenderloin registers 130˚F (55ºC).
» Once at the target temperature, remove from the barbecue and let stand at room temperature for 30 minutes. Cover and chill in the refrigerator for 12–24 hours.
» Take the cooking plate out of the now cold barbecue. Coat the cold cooking plate grill with olive oil cooking spray. Preheat grill to a high heat 400˚–450˚F (190º–210ºC). Once the temperature is reached, replace cooking plate—be careful, use gloves.
» Place the chilled tenderloin on the cooking plate and grill until the whole surface is seared for about 4–5 minutes. Remove meat from heat and let it rest for 5 minutes.
» Serve very thinly sliced.

NOTE This goes well with Murphy's Ranch Dressing (page 173, Quick Barbecue Sauce (page 154) or Horseradish Mustard Sauce (page 166). You can cook this without the 12- to 24-hour chill time, but this isn't recommended if you like your beef rare.

• •

CHICKEN FRIED RIB-EYE STEAK

Serves 4

• •

Everybody has heard of chicken-fried steaks, normally made with round steak. When you use top-quality boneless rib-eye steak, it takes the chicken-fried steak to a whole new level of deliciousness.

INGREDIENTS

2 large eggs

8 fl oz (250 ml) milk

4 x 12 oz (375 g), boneless rib-eye steaks, 1½ inch (3 cm) thick, fat trimmed and tenderized

8 oz (250 g) all-purpose (plain) flour

1 tablespoon garlic salt

1 tablespoon onion salt

1 teaspoon black pepper

dash of cumin

dash of paprika, hot, sweet or smoked

6 tablespoons extra virgin olive oil, for frying

Texan White Gravy (page 172), to serve

METHOD

» Whisk eggs and milk together in a large bowl and place tenderized steaks in one at a time.

» Mix flour, salt and spices together in a covered plastic container or a zip-lock plastic bag and shake thoroughly. Place on a large plate.

» Remove the steak from the egg mixture and generously coat steaks in the flour mix.

» Heat oil in a frypan on the barbecue or stove top. Test the oil with a pinch of flour. When the flour starts to bubble, it is ready. Fry the rib-eye steak until golden brown on one side. Then, and only then, turn over and cook the other side.

» Drain on a wire rack, pat with a paper towel and add some salt while steaks are still hot.

» Serve with Texan White Gravy (page 172).

NOTE For this recipe, you can use sirloin, skirt or round steak. Make sure that these cuts are tenderized.

• •

DR PEPPER RIBS

Serves 6

* *

The soft drink Dr Pepper was originally sold as a medicine even though it has no medicinal value whatsoever. It just makes you feel better, probably because of the sugar hit. It is not really sold as a marinade, but it makes a surprisingly tasty marinade when combined with a few other things. This version of beef short ribs is hard to beat.

INGREDIENTS

6 beef rib racks, cut 1 inch (2½ cm) thick
2 batches Dr Pepper Marinade (page 177)
3 tablespoons maple syrup
6 tablespoons water

salt and freshly ground black pepper, to taste
Quick Barbecue Sauce (page 154), to serve
mayonnaise or aioli (optional), to serve

METHOD

» Place rib racks in a large plastic container or in a zip-lock plastic bag and add one batch of Dr Pepper Marinade to cover. Leave in the refrigerator for 3 hours or preferably overnight.
» Wrap the ribs tightly in tin foil and cook at 225°–250°F (100°–125°C) away from direct heat on your barbecue for at least an hour.
» Unwrap the ribs and dip them into the fresh (second batch) marinade. Set them directly over the fire until they are a deep reddish-brown with a crust on both sides.
» Combine maple syrup and warm water in a small bowl to make a glaze. Lightly brush the surface of the cooked ribs with the glaze and season the ribs lightly with salt and pepper.
» Serve with barbecue sauce, mayonnaise/aioli or any other favorite sauce or condiment.

NOTE This dish can be served whole to serve 6 people as a main, or cut each section in half and serve 12 as a starter. If you really must use ribs 'off the rack', they will be three times larger than this recipe requires. This will affect the cooking times and will involve cooking the wrapped ribs very slowly on a low, indirect heat until the internal meat temperature is about 180°F (80°C).

STEAK SANDWICHES

Serves 6

* *

This is the king of steak sandwiches. If you want a tender steak sandwich that you can bite through with no problem, this is it—melt-in-the-mouth stuff.

INGREDIENTS

2 lb (1 kg) flank (skirt) steak, trimmed and tenderized

2 teaspoons extra virgin olive oil

1 tablespoon unsalted butter

1 teaspoon Dijon mustard

2 teaspoons salt

2 teaspoons coarsely ground black pepper

12 slices bread, cut thickly

Horseradish Mustard Sauce (page 166)

1 small head cos lettuce

2 medium tomatoes, sliced thinly

salt and freshly ground black pepper, to taste

unsalted butter, for spreading

METHOD

» Preheat the barbecue to medium-high heat, 400°F (200°C).

» Lightly brush the beef with olive oil. Mix the unsalted butter and mustard together in a small bowl and spread the mixture over the beef with your hands. Sprinkle the meat evenly with the salt and pepper. Bring the meat to room temperature.

» Place on a well-oiled barbecue grill over a medium-high heat and cook for 4–5 minutes on each side or until meat is medium rare. Remove from the grill and allow it to rest on a wire rack for 5–7 minutes before cutting the steak into strips.

» Spread six of the bread slices thickly with the horseradish mustard sauce. Top with slices of beef, lettuce and tomato and sprinkle with salt and pepper.

» Spread the other 6 slices of bread with butter and place on top to form sandwiches.

» Cut diagonally and serve while still warm.

NOTE Try a different sauce by whisking together mayonnaise, mustard of choice, horseradish, sour cream and a pinch of salt in a small bowl. Add tasty cheddar or other favorite cheese and/or cucumber slices (not many) and thinly sliced red bell peppers. If you have a smoker, you can use the resting time to gently cool smoke (at less than 170ºF or 77ºC) the meat with some fruit wood to add a very pleasant flavor.

* *

REVERSE SEARED TOMAHAWK STEAKS

Serves 4

* *

This is the most fun you can have with a steak. Kids love these because they can use the bone handle and gnaw on them.

INGREDIENTS

4 bone-in rib-eye steaks, 1½–2 inch (3.75–5 cm) thick, 6–10 inch (15–25 cm) bone handle (ask your butcher to cut these for you)

extra virgin olive oil, for cooking

salt and freshly ground black pepper, to taste

2 oz (60 g) garlic or herb butter (optional), to serve

METHOD

» Brush steaks lightly with olive oil. Season with salt and pepper and place in the refrigerator for at least 2 hours.

» Preheat your barbecue or grill to a medium-high heat, 400°F (200°C).

» Remove steaks from the refrigerator and rest for 20–30 minutes at room temperature.

» Using indirect heat, cook the steak slowly at about 10°F (5°C) lower than its target temperature (see page 22). It is very important that you have a meat thermometer to check the temperature properly. When the meat reaches the 10 degrees below mark, brush the outside with oil and lightly sprinkle both sides with a coarse mixture of salt and pepper, only then are the steaks ready for the final sear.

» Once the steak is at that lower 10 degree point, move the steak immediately to direct heat, (for example, over coals) to sear for an excellent charred crust. This should only take a couple of minutes on each side, and the meat should reach the desired temperature during that time.

» Once seared, remove the meat and rest for 5–7 minutes.

» Serve hot with a knob of garlic or herb butter on each steak.

NOTE Do not overcook these steaks. Check the internal temperature a few minutes before the suggested cooking time. Using red-hot charcoals can take less time, however, cooking low and slow allows the meat to cook evenly and locks in the flavor. Some people are always looking to add a sauce no matter how good something tastes. This dish shouldn't need it. If you do, try some Horseradish Mustard Sauce (page 166), or a bit of Worcestershire sauce.

* *

BEEF

TEXAN T-BONE

Serves 4

* *

T-bone is the king of steaks in Texas and other parts of the world too. There are thousands of spice rub combinations for T-bone steaks. You can use a rub or marinade, but the traditional Texas recipe is made with good cooking oil and seasoned with salt and pepper. The idea is to get the full flavor of the beef. Ask your butcher to cut the steaks to 1½–2 inch (3.75–5 cm) thick and no smaller than 16 oz (500 g) each, trimmed. Ask for the fat to be trimmed to ¼ inch (6 mm) thickness.

INGREDIENTS
4 T-bone steaks
extra virgin olive oil, for cooking

salt and freshly ground black pepper, to taste
barbecue sauce (optional), to serve

METHOD
» Rub the T-bone steaks with oil. Season with salt and pepper and press into each steak. Cover and refrigerate for 1 hour. Let the steak stand at room temperature for 20–30 minutes before cooking.
» Build a wood fire, heat coals, or heat the barbecue grill for direct heat. If you prefer to reverse sear, see page 22. Reverse sear works best on these thick steaks. Use low and slow indirect heat or smoking. this will take about 35–45 minutes of indirect heat. To be certain, remove when the internal temperature is 10 degrees below the target temperature.
» Cook on direct heat for about 2 minutes on each side and it should be perfect.
» Sprinkle with additional salt and pepper as desired. Rest your steaks for 7–10 minutes.
» Serve with a good-quality barbecue sauce or sauce and condiments of your choice.

NOTE When cooking top-quality beef such as T-bone, I like to use just salt and pepper. If the steaks don't look great, try a rub or a marinade before cooking, or use some of my Texas Cowboy Barbecue Sauce (page 161).

* *

Beauty

BEEF

STEAK FAJITAS

Serves 4–6

Fajitas (pronounced *far-heata*) is a popular dish from the Tex-Mex cuisine. For the very best tender fajitas, use skirt (flank) steak. This is the cut originally used and it's perfect—it cooks easily and tastes better than anything else. In the Mexican ranching states that share a border with Texas, a similar dish called *arracheras* (grilled fillets of skirt steak) has been served for decades.

INGREDIENTS

1–2 lb (½–1 kg) skirt (flank) steak, trimmed
1 batch Fajitas Marinade (page 178)
2 tablespoons extra virgin olive oil
1 green bell pepper (capsicum), sliced into strips lengthwise
1 red bell pepper (capsicum), sliced into strips lengthwise
1 yellow bell peppers (capsicum), sliced into strips lengthwise

2 medium onions, halved, cut into ½ inch (7 cm) wide strips
pinch of salt
6 x 6 inch (15 cm) flour tortillas, warmed
4 tablespoons sour cream, to serve
1 can refried beans, to serve
Pico de Gallo (page 127), to serve
Roasted Salsa (page 169), to serve
avocado or guacamole, to serve

METHOD

» Marinate the steak in the marinade in a zip-lock plastic bag in the refrigerator for at least 8 hours and for up to 24 hours. Turn occasionally for maximum coverage.
» Remove from the refrigerator and allow the steak to reach room temperature, about 20 minutes.
» Preheat your barbecue or grill to a medium-high heat, 400°F (200°C).
» Remove the steak from the marinade and place on an oiled grill . Grill 3–4 minutes each side for medium.
» Place the steak on a clean cutting board and let rest for 5–7 minutes.
» While resting the steak, add 1 tablespoon of olive oil to a large frypan and put on the barbecue over high heat until the oil is shimmering. Add peppers and onion strips. Sprinkle with salt and cook, stirring, until vegetables are blackened in spots and just softened, about 4–6 minutes.
» Cut meat into 1 inch (2½ cm) slices across the grain—this helps keep the steak tender.
» Serve the steak and vegetables on a platter with the warmed tortillas so everyone can fill the tortillas and make their fajitas to their liking.
» Serve with bowls of sour cream, refried beans, Pico de Gallo (page 127), salsa (pages 169–172) and avocado/ guacamole—any combination will work.

NOTE Old El Paso is a reputable brand of refried beans that is available in supermarkets around the world. There are many variations of condiments for Fajitas. Feel free to use your imagination.

TEXAS STYLE BRISKET

Serves 12–15

* *

This recipe takes time, but it is *totally* worth it. You will need a barbecue with an offset smoker and some wood for smoking: hickory, oak, mesquite (ironbark will work a bit), pecan or any of the fruitwoods. Make sure you have a meat temperature gauge and a good supply of tin foil. This is my favorite thing to cook and serve!

INGREDIENTS

11–14 lb (5–6 kg) brisket (point only)
4 oz (125 g) salt
8 oz (250 g) coarse-ground pepper
extra virgin olive oil, for cooking

24 slices bread, white or of choice
butter, for spreading
barbecue sauce (optional), to serve

METHOD

» Trim some of the fat off the brisket and shape the brisket to be aerodynamic. Rinse and pat dry, then oil it. Combine salt and pepper and rub the mixture on all sides. Wrap in clear wrap and place in the refrigerator overnight or for at least 4–5 hours.

» Preheat your barbecue (with offset smoker) to 250ºF (125ºC)—the smoker needs to be between 150º–170ºF (65º–77ºC).

» Place the brisket fat-side-up in the smoker with the large end towards the firebox, and smoke it until the desired color (dark brown but not black) is reached, about 3–5 hours.

» Remove from the smoker and wrap tightly in tin foil and place in the cooking part (indirect heat) of your barbecue but not in the firebox. Cook at around 250ºF (120ºC) for another 7–10 hours, depending on thickness, outside temperature, wind, type of wood, humidity and composition of the meat tissue. The brisket is done when the internal meat temperature is at 190ºF (88ºC).

» The brisket will be black when it comes out of the barbecue—it looks like a meteorite has just landed.

» Remove the brisket from smoker and let rest for 20–40 minutes until the temperature of the brisket is 145ºF (63ºC).

» Cut the brisket across the grain and serve with bread and butter, barbecue sauce or other favorite sauces or condiments.

NOTE Use the brisket to create other dishes such as Brisket Sandwiches (page 57) or you can serve it on Texan Toast (page 128). For more tips on smoking brisket, see page 23. There are other methods for cooking smaller briskets that take less time and you can also cook these in the oven. However, the best smoky flavor is achieved from a larger sized brisket smoked on a barbecue.

* *

BRISKET SANDWICHES WITH SPICY BARBECUE SAUCE

Serves 8-12

* *

After you've cooked the Texas Style Brisket (page 52), the hard part is over. Now you can make delicious sandwiches.

INGREDIENTS

2–3 lb (½–1½ kg) cooked brisket (4 oz/125 g per person)
4 tablespoons Beef Stock (page 153)
4 tablespoons Quick Barbecue Sauce (page 161)
½ teaspoon salt
½ teaspoon pepper

8–12 hamburger buns, lightly toasted
1 white onion, sliced
8–12 dill pickles, sliced
4 tablespoons mayonnaise
condiments of choice, to serve
potato crisps, to serve

METHOD

» Chop the brisket with the fat still on. Place in a bowl with stock and barbecue sauce and mix. Add salt and pepper to taste. Add more sauce as necessary.

» Place brisket mix on a serving dish and arrange all other ingredients on serving platters for your guests to make their own sandwiches.

» Serve your favorite sauces such as ketchup, extra barbecue sauce and/or mustard, and potato crisps on the side.

NOTE These sandwiches go very well with beer, root beer or cola. You can also make sliced brisket sandwiches using white bread.

* *

BEEF

TEXAS STYLE MEATLOAF

Serves 6

The reason meatloaf has stayed around for so many centuries? It's continually evolving. It works for everybody. Germans put *whole* boiled eggs inside theirs, the Romans made theirs with wine-soaked bread and spices. People in medieval Europe served it mixed with nuts and seasonings. You can add any of the above or just about anything you want to your meatloaf.

INGREDIENTS

3 large eggs
4 fl oz (125 ml) Beef Stock (page 153)
4 fl oz (125 ml) ketchup
1½ tablespoons mustard
2 teaspoons Worcestershire Sauce
8 oz (225 g) tomato purée
salt and pepper, to taste
16 oz (500 g) premium ground beef (mince)

10–15 crackers, crushed or 6 oz (175 g) breadcrumbs
1 medium onion, chopped
½ green bell pepper (capsicum), chopped, seeds and stem removed
2 jalapeños, diced, seeds removed
2 garlic cloves, chopped
2–3 streaky bacon, thin strips, crispy fried, then crumbled

METHOD

» Preheat barbecue or oven to 350°–375°F (180°–190°C).
» Beat the eggs then mix together with the stock, ketchup, mustard, Worcestershire and half the tomato purée. Season to taste.
» Place ground beef in a bowl with the crackers or breadcrumbs. Add onion, bell pepper, jalapeños, garlic and bacon. Pour in the egg mixture and blend together thoroughly.
» Pour into an oiled meatloaf tray (about 8 x 14 inch/20 x 35 cm) then spread evenly. Cover the meatloaf with the rest of the tomato purée.
» Cook on a covered barbecue (indirect heat) or in the oven for 35–45 minutes until done (internal temperature of 170°F/77°C). If cooking on the barbecue, uncover and cook for a further 5 minutes to brown on top.
» Serve hot with your favorite sauce/condiment such as barbecue, ketchup, mayonnaise or mustard.

NOTE Save some to make sandwiches the next day (meatloaf and Swiss cheese on grilled rye is excellent) or shepherd's pie (with mashed potato and dobs of butter on top) or serve in corn tortillas with sour cream and salsa of your choice (pages 169–172)—endless choices for this versatile dish.

SLOW COOKED BEEF RIBS

Serves 8

* *

Most people stay away from beef ribs because they are tough and hard to cook correctly. Try this method of oven-baked short ribs or cook over indirect heat on a hooded barbecue.

INGREDIENTS

4½ lb (2 kg) beef rib racks, cut into 3 inch (7.5 cm) pieces

1 tablespoon mustard (optional)

1 tablespoon ketchup (optional)

2–4 tablespoons extra virgin olive oil

salt and pepper, to taste

1 batch Beef Rib Rub (page 187)

4 fl oz (125 ml) Quick Barbecue Sauce (page 154)

1 tablespoon brown sugar (optional)

spices of choice (optional)

METHOD

» Rinse ribs and pat dry with paper towels.

» Coat dry ribs with mustard or ketchup mixed in with olive oil (optional) or just lightly coat in extra virgin olive oil.

» Season generously with salt and pepper, front and back.

» Rub the Beef Rib Rub into the ribs.

» Place the ribs in a large zip-lock plastic bag or covered bowl and marinate (with dry rub only) in the fridge for at least 1–2 hours or up to 24 hours.

» Preheat the barbecue or oven to 250°F (125°C).

» Place the ribs on a foil-lined baking tray in a single layer.

» Add another piece of foil on top and seal the edges tightly so that no steam can escape while cooking

» Bake in a covered barbecue or on the middle rack of the oven for 3–3½ hours. Visually check after 2 hours. The oven temperature is very low so you can cook it a bit longer without overcooking.

» When the ribs start to pull away, or 190°F (84°C) is reached, drain off the excess fat.

» Brush the ribs with desired amount of barbecue sauce.

» Broil (grill) on low until the sauce starts to glaze.

» Uncover on the barbecue and sprinkle some brown sugar or spices on top, but try them first, you may not need this.

» Serve hot or warm.

NOTE The ribs will be more tender if they reach the temperature of 190°F (84°C) before you put the glaze on—the best way to achieve the right temperature is to use your meat thermometer.

* *

STEAK AND LOBSTER SLIDERS

Makes 12

* *

These are a little tricky to make and assemble but much easier once you get the hang of it.

INGREDIENTS

20 oz (550 g) sirloin steak
extra virgin olive oil, for cooking
6 small lobster tails, shells on, cut in half lengthwise
1 batch Black Butter Sauce (page 155)

12 small, oval dinner rolls, cut in half not all the way
  through (butterflied)
12 baby cos lettuce leaves, washed and pat dried
9 oz (250 g) cream cheese

METHOD

» Preheat barbecue grill to medium high heat, 400°F (200°C).
» Allow the steak to come to room temperature. Trim off fat and cut into thin strips. Add olive oil to a frypan (to cook on the barbecue) and lightly sauté the sirloin strips over medium heat until sealed but still rare. Set aside.
» To pre-cook the lobster tails, firstly make 6 lobster tail boats. Cut two sheets of tin foil, approximately 12 inch (30 cm) square, for each lobster tail. Put the two layers together for each and turn up the sides to create boats.
» Place lobster tails, shell side down, in lobster tail boats. Pour the butter sauce on top of lobster tails, evenly distributed until half the sauce is used up.
» Place lobster boats on barbecue grill on direct heat and cook for 3–4 minutes. The meat will change color from translucent to solid white. Brush lobster with some of the remaining butter sauce.
» While lobsters are cooking, toast butterflied rolls on grill for about 2 minutes with tops up.
» Brush grill with a little oil then immediately take lobster tail halves out of their boats and place flesh-side down onto grill over direct heat. Cook for 20 to 60 seconds.
» Remove tails immediately from heat. Remove lobster flesh immediately from shells and cut each half lobster tail into half again, lengthwise so that you have 12 pieces of lobster tail.
» To assemble each slider, take a cos lettuce leaf, spread with cream cheese. Place a lobster tail quarter on top of the cheese, then add sirloin strips on top of the lobster.
» Place entire assembly in a roll and serve immediately. Alternatively, let everyone assemble their own slider.

NOTE For an easy version of butter sauce, just use butter with garlic and salt and forget about making the Black Butter Sauce. For a main meal, you can allow 2 sliders per person to serve 6. Very filling! You can use shrimp (prawns) or any lobster-like ocean-going bug cooked in a little garlic butter or black butter sauce as desired. If you make double the Black Butter Sauce, store half in the freezer for up to 8 weeks.

* *

TEXAS STYLE PRIME RIB

Serves 15

* *

Prime rib is the ultimate roasted meat. I suggest you cook this with the bone in and remove after cooking (the bone adds flavor).

INGREDIENTS

9–13½ lb (4–6 kg) prime ribs (standing rib roast), bone removed
Prime Rib Rub (page 188)

1 tablespoon extra virgin olive oil (optional)
4–6 fl oz (125–200 ml) Beef Stock (page 153)

METHOD

» Preheat the barbecue to high or 500°F (250°C).
» Rub the meat with the Prime Rib Rub. If necessary, add some olive oil to help it stick to the surface.
» Place the roast on a wire rack in a roasting pan and pour in the stock. Roast for 45 minutes (indirect heat), then decrease the temperature to 350°F (175° C) and roast until cooled to your liking by checking with a meat thermometer (see page 23).
» Remove from barbecue and rest for 10–15 minutes.
» Slice the meat and place on serving dish. Pour over with meat drippings.
» Serve with your favorite condiments.

NOTE If you buy the rib roast with the bone, you can remove it before serving. After you remove the bone, cook the meat over direct heat of your barbecue grill for a few minutes before resting it. This goes well with barbecue sauce, ketchup, mayonnaise, your favorite mustard or any other condiment of choice.

* *

Chapter 2
LAMB AND PORK

LAMB CUTLETS

Serves 6

* *

Lamb rib chops are like tiny, thick-cut T-bone steaks. These will cost you but, boy, are they good when cooked properly. Here's one way that's hard to mess up.

INGREDIENTS

12 lamb cutlets, 1¼–1½ inch (3–4 cm) thick

3 tablespoons extra virgin olive oil

1 batch Easy Lamb Rub (page 191) or Lamb Rub
 (page 191)

12 roasted baby potatoes

24 baby carrots, steamed

yogurt dipping sauce, to serve

Honey Mustard Sauce (page 162), to serve

METHOD

» Trim the cutlets of any hard fat or gristle.

» Coat cutlets with olive oil and sprinkle the rub on both sides of the cutlets. Rub in well (about 30 minutes before you cook). Allow the cutlets to come to room temperature.

» Preheat barbecue to medium high, 400°F (200°C).

» Cook cutlets over direct heat for 4–6 minutes. Alternatively, use the reverse sear method by cooking in a covered, slightly-oiled foil tray on indirect heat until the internal temperature is 120°F (52°C), then remove from tray and cook over direct heat for about 1–1½ minutes to add a crispy charred outside—at the internal target temperature of 130°F (54°C).

» Allow to rest for 5–7 minutes and serve with roasted baby potatoes and steamed baby carrots. Serve with yogurt dipping sauce and honey mustard sauce on the side.

NOTE You can cook these in the oven and finish them off with a reverse sear by
using the broiler (grill) if you wish.

* *

LAMB RIBS

Serves 8

• •

Lamb ribs are so good—really, there's nothing more to say.

INGREDIENTS

4 tablespoons lemon juice

2 oz (50 g) extra virgin olive oil

2 tablespoons fresh oregano

2 sprigs thyme, roughly chopped

2 cloves garlic, minced

2 fl oz (60 ml) maple syrup or molasses

2 tablespoons brown sugar

2 fl oz (60 ml) warm water

2 four-bone racks of lamb (each 8 oz (500 g)

potato salad, to serve

sprigs of rosemary, to serve

METHOD

» Thoroughly mix together lemon juice, oil, oregano, thyme, garlic, maple syrup, brown sugar and water to make the marinade. Set aside.

» Trim lamb ribs of fat and remove the silverskin. Place ribs in a large sealable bag with the marinade making sure the ribs are completely covered. Place in refrigerator, preferably overnight or for at least 2 hours. Remove and allow to come to room temperature, about 20 minutes.

» If using a smoker, preheat your smoker to at least 170°F (77°C) with fruitwood. Add the ribs to the smoker and cook for 1–2 hours.

» If using a barbecue, preheat to 325°F (163°C). Cover the ribs in aluminum foil pan and cook on indirect heat for 30–40 minutes at or until they are tender and the meat starts to pull away from the bone. Open the foil and brush the glaze lightly on the surface.

» Cook for another 10–20 minutes on indirect heat until the desired color is achieved or for a few minutes on direct heat on your barbecue grill, fat side down for a more charred result. The internal temperature is 135°F (57°C) for medium. Rest for 3–6 minutes.

» Carve and lightly salt. Garnish with sprigs of rosemary and serve with potato salad or other salad of choice.

• •

LAMB STEAK AND EGG BURRITO

Serves 4

* *

In South Texas and Mexico, meat and red beans are sometimes the only fillings for burritos. In the United States and other parts of the world, burrito fillings can include a combination of ingredients such as brown, saffron, white rice, beans, refried beans, cilantro (coriander), lettuce, salsa, chicken, beef or pork, guacamole, cheese and sour cream. This is a great 'road food' because there is less chance for you to make a mess. The folded bit on the bottom keeps the contents from spilling, so you can eat burritos with one hand. The size of burritos can vary. What makes a burrito is *the way it is folded*. This lamb steak and egg version should get you started on your burrito journey.

INGREDIENTS

2 tablespoons butter

2 medium onions or a small red onion, thinly sliced

4 lamb skirt steaks or rib eye steaks, 8 oz (250 g) each, no bone

salt and pepper, to taste

4 eggs

½ tablespoon milk

8 fl oz (250 ml) sour cream

8 extra large flour tortillas, about 12 inch (30 cm)

12 oz (375 g) iceberg lettuce, shredded

oil for brushing and warming tortillas

Tabasco sauce (optional), to taste

hot sauce (optional), to taste

METHOD

» In a large frypan (or on the barbecue plate), heat the butter over medium heat. Add in the onions and cook until deep brown and caramelized for about 15–20 minutes. Season with salt and pepper and set aside.

» Heat the barbecue grill to medium high, 400°F (200°C).

» Sprinkle the steaks liberally with salt and pepper. Cook over direct heat until medium rare, about 4–5 minutes per side. Remove and set aside to rest for 5–7 minutes.

» Crack the eggs in a large pan and add some milk. Season to taste. Mix to make scrambled eggs and set aside.

» While the meat is resting, put the sour cream, scrambled egg and lettuce into separate serving bowls then warm the tortillas. Place on a serving plate.

» Slice the rested steak into 1 inch (2½ cm) strips and place on a serving plate.

» Line up the plates and bowls on a serving space: burritos first, then lamb steak, egg, lettuce, sour cream and sauces so that guests can assemble their own burritos.

NOTE Add cheese and salsa if you wish. All burritos go very well with salsa (pages 169–172).

* *

EASY PORK RIB SHINERS

Serves 8

* *

This is an easy recipe partly because you can use the standard pork ribs you get from the supermarket. They are tasty and full of flavor when cooked well.

INGREDIENTS

2 racks pork ribs, about 8 lb (4 kg)

meat tenderizer (papain) or 12 fl oz (375 ml) milk

1 batch Pork Rib Rub (page 192)

1 teaspoon garlic salt

1 teaspoon onion salt

ground black pepper, to taste

1 batch Quick Barbecue Sauce (page 154), to serve

METHOD

» Remove any excess fat or gristle from the rib racks. Detach the silverskin and remove from both racks.

» Place racks in a shallow baking dish and sprinkle with meat tenderizer or pour over with the milk. Cover and place in the refrigerator for at least 1–2 hours. Remove from refrigerator and pat dry with paper towels.

» Take a sharp fork and stab holes in the rib meat. Place the ribs in a sealable plastic bag or plastic container and cover with half the rub. Shake to make sure ribs are covered and place in the refrigerator overnight.

» Preheat barbecue to 300°F (150°C).

» Remove the ribs from the refrigerator and allow to come to room temperature.

» Cook in a covered baking dish for 50 minutes to 1 hour or until 180°F (82°C) internal temperature is reached. Remove from the heat, uncover and add the other half of the rub seasoning, garlic salt, onion salt and pepper.

» Cook for about another 10 minutes on the barbecue or under a broiler (grill), turning to cook on both sides. When they have a nice color and texture, the bone should start to pull away and the outside should have a nice crust.

» Serve hot or warm with barbecue sauce.

* *

BARBECUED PORK CHOPS

Serves 6

* *

Start with your new best friend, your butcher, and ask for rib chops. These are the best. You can think of these as being like small bone-in rib-eye steaks. If you pick the wrong cut of chop, it won't be as tender or flavorsome, so make sure you get the right ones. Start right and finish right.

INGREDIENTS

6 pork rib chops, 1 inch (3 cm) thick
extra virgin olive oil, for cooking

salt and pepper, to taste
1 batch Red Wine Mustard Sauce (page 162)

METHOD

» Preheat barbecue to medium high, 400°F (200°C).
» Allow the chops to come to room temperature before cooking. Rub some oil on the surface of each. Add some salt and pepper to the surface of the chops and place the chops on the barbecue grill about 5 inch (13 cm) from the flame or coals.
» Cook for 6–7 minutes on each side on medium heat. Render the fat on the chops by holding them with tongs, fat-side-down directly over the hottest part of the grill surface for about 2 minutes. The high heat initially helps these to have a charred, golden and crispy outside.
» During the cooking, every minute or so, brush with the sauce. Cook to an internal meat temperature of 145°F (63°C).
» Remove from heat and rest for 8–10 minutes.
» Serve with the remaining sauce on the side.

NOTE The reverse sear method also works well when cooking these rib chops. Do not be afraid to use more salt and pepper on pork chops while cooking, it helps create a crusty exterior.

* *

BARBECUED PINEAPPLE HAM

Serves 15

∗ ∗

You can look like the greatest cook of all time and not have to do much with this recipe. It is already cooked—all you have to do is make it look and taste incredible. Here's how.

INGREDIENTS

15–20 lb (7–9 kg) fully cooked ham
4 fl oz (125 ml) maple syrup
3–4 tablespoons American mustard
8 fl oz (250 ml) sliced pineapple, canned
4 oz (125 g) red glacé cherries

2 fl oz (60 ml) pineapple juice (from canned
  pineapple)
2 fl oz (60 ml) of water
fruitwood, for smoking
Honey Mustard Sauce (page 162)

METHOD

» Preheat your barbecue to medium high, 400°F (200°C). The fire should be burned down to a nice bed of coals. Turn the barbecue to 250º–300ºF (120º–140ºC) in preparation for cooking the ham and make sure you have your fruitwood handy for smoking.

» Remove the outside of the skin of the ham and score the fat (not too deep) diagonally.

» Mix your maple syrup and mustard together to form a glaze.

» Rub the glaze all over the outside of the ham.

» Place your glazed ham on a heavy-duty aluminum foil pan. Arrange your sliced pineapples over the top of the ham.

» Skewer cherries with toothpicks and place them in the middle of pineapple slices to secure the slices in place.

» Pour about half the reserved pineapple juice and water in the bottom of the foil pan. This pineapple juice and water will cook out and steam the ham which will keep it moist.

» Get your barbecue smoking with some fruitwood.

» Place your ham in the foil pan on your barbecue over indirect heat and close the lid. Cook for approximately 35 minutes. All you want to do is 'heat up' the ham and bring out the flavor of the glaze. Remove from heat and allow to cool a little.

» Serve whole at the table as it will look so beautiful you won't want to cut it, but go ahead, because it will taste as good as it looks.

» Serve with the honey mustard sauce and/or your favorite condiments.

NOTE You can also place a pan of water between the fire and what you are smoking to help keep the meat moist. Alternatively, you can cook this in your oven, just don't try to smoke it. It will still look and taste great.

∗ ∗

GOAT SAUSAGES

Makes 35-40 sausages

* *

OK, this isn't 100 percent pork, but it's so good I had to include it.

INGREDIENTS

5 lb (2 kg) goat mince

2 lb (1 kg) pork mince (chemically lean 'CL' or 40% fat)

2 lb (1 kg) beef mince

3 oz (100 g) black pepper

4 oz (125 g) salt

3 sprigs rosemary

40 standard 23-gauge clear sausage casings, (optional if butcher makes these)

METHOD

» Tell your butcher that you're planning to smoke sausages. Show the above recipe and ask if your butcher will fill the sausages for you—find out which days they make sausages and they won't mind. It shouldn't cost you much more than what they'd normally charge for the ingredients on their own.

» Preheat your barbecue smoker to 170°F (77°C) and begin smoking with fruitwood.

» Hang your sausages in the smoker so that the smoke can cover the entire surface of the sausages. The smoking area temperature should be at least 170°F (77°C).

» Close the smoker and maintain the smoke and heat at relatively the same temperature. When the sausages turn to a medium brown color they are probably done. This will take about 1 to 1½ hours depending on the weather, wood and other conditions. Cut into one sausage to see if it is cooked. They'll look kind of gray but still moist. Don't overcook them as they will be too dry. Remove from smoker and allow to cool.

» Use sausages for sandwiches, breakfast, pizzas, hot dogs and even sausage rolls.

NOTE These sausages have a mild flavor and will last for quite a while.

* *

PIG SIDE

Serves 20

* *

If you are having a party, take this with you. See your butcher about this cut, which is also known as Pork Belly, as it's not the whole half; the shoulder and hindquarter is not attached.

INGREDIENTS

12 fl oz (375 ml) Beef Stock (page 153)
2 apples, sliced
2–3 white onions, sliced
2–3 celery stalks, chopped
1 side of pig
2 fl oz (60 ml) extra virgin olive oil
2–4 tablespoons sea salt flakes
2–4 tablespoons freshly ground black pepper

1 tablespoon onion salt
1 tablespoon garlic salt
2 tablespoons maple syrup
2 tablespoons honey
1 tablespoon brown sugar
4 tablespoons hot water
barbecue sauce

METHOD

» Preheat barbecue to 500ºF (250ºC).
» Pour stock into a large roasting pan with apple, onion and celery.
» Score pork skin with diagonal cross-hatch cuts. Rub in half the oil. Mix together salt, pepper, onion and garlic salt and press into the scored skin.
» Place pork, skin-side up, into the roasting pan.
» Cook uncovered at a high heat (indirect) until you have a good color and the skin is becoming crispy.
» Turn pork, skin-side down, decrease barbecue temperature to 250˚–300˚F (120˚–140˚C). Bake for 1–2 hours. Check to make sure skin is crispy. Remove from barbecue and wrap with foil.
» Return to barbecue and cook until internal meat temperature is 190ºF (90ºC), about another 2–3 hours.
» Mix maple syrup, honey and brown sugar with hot water and brush on top of the pork.
» Place the pork back onto the barbecue on indirect high heat, skin-side up until skin is glazed and crispy. If you are using an oven, put the pork under the broiler for a few minutes. Remove and allow to cool for a few minutes.
» Thickly slice pork and serve.

NOTE To check the temperature, insert the meat thermometer into the thickest part of the meat away from the bone. The meat should be cooked for about 1 hour for every 2 lb (1 kg) at 375ºF (180ºC).

* *

CRISPY SMOKED PORK LOIN CHOPS

Serves 6

* *

Start with the pork loin chops. Look at the label on the package or, better yet, ask your butcher. The more you know about what you are cooking, the better you'll be able to cook it. There are different cuts of pork chops, some better than others. Pork loin chops are the best all round.

INGREDIENTS

6 pork loin chops (pork steaks)
1 batch Pork Loin Marinade (page 182)
fruitwood, for smoking
2 oz (60 g) all-purpose (plain) flour
1 teaspoon onion salt
2 medium eggs

1 tablespoons milk
4 oz (125 g) cheese crackers, crushed (or Panko breadcrumbs)
1 teaspoon cayenne pepper
extra virgin olive oil, for cooking
Honey Mustard Sauce (page 162), to serve

METHOD

» Place the loin chops in a sealable plastic container with the marinade ensuring chops are completely covered. Refrigerate overnight or for 3–5 hours. Allow chops to come to room temperature before cooking, about 20 minutes.

» Preheat barbecue to 250°F (120°C) and add fruitwood for smoking.

» Place chops on indirect heat on barbecue. Smoke for up to an hour, turning once during the process until chops are medium. If you don't have a smoker, just cook them to medium on 250°F (120°C). Set chops aside and cover.

» Mix the flour with onion salt and put on a plate. Whisk together eggs and milk and put in a shallow bowl. Mix crushed crackers with cayenne pepper and put on a plate. Dip the warm chops in that order so that chops are coated.

» Heat oil to high in a large, deep skillet and flash-fry until chops are golden and crispy on the outside, 2–3 minutes at the most. Allow to rest for 5–7 minutes.

» Serve with Honey Mustard Sauce.

NOTE Pork should be cooked until the internal temperature at the thickest part of the meat reaches 145°F (63°C) degrees. As the chops continue to cook past this point, they become increasingly tough and leathery so avoid overcooking. Also, don't be shy about seasoning pork—it will improve the taste.

* *

VENISON SAUSAGE WITH OMELET AND BACON SANDWICH

Serves 10

* *

Not lamb or pork, but still great if you can get your hands on some venison.

INGREDIENTS

Venison Sausage
16 oz (500 g) ground venison
16 oz (500 g) ground pork mince
1 teaspoon sage
2 teaspoons marjoram
2 teaspoons thyme
2 teaspoons red chili flakes, to taste
½ teaspoon cayenne pepper
2 teaspoons brown sugar
salt and freshly ground black pepper
extra virgin olive oil (optional)

1 egg (optional)
2 tablespoons Dijonnaise

Omelet
12 medium eggs
6 fl oz (200 ml) milk
5 oz (150 ml) cream
2 tablespoons olive oil
½ red bell pepper (capsicum), diced
½ yellow bell pepper (capsicum), diced
½ bunch cilantro (coriander),

chopped
½ red onion, diced
16 oz (250 g) 3 different cheeses of choice

Sandwich
10 pieces streaky bacon, fried until crispy
20 slices ciabatta bread
10 iceberg lettuce leaves
salt and pepper, to taste

METHOD

» To make the sausage, mix all the ingredients thoroughly. Add olive oil or use an egg for binding if needed. Roll into palm-sized meatballs (makes about 10–12).
» Preheat barbecue plate to medium high, 400˚F (200˚C). Add olive oil to the hotplate then add meatballs and crush into patties. Cook halfway through then turn and cook the other side. Drain on paper towels and place on a wire rack. Set aside and rest for 2–3 minutes.
» To cook the omelet, preheat the barbecue (or oven) to 250º–275ºF (130º–140ºC).
» In a large bowl, whisk eggs, milk and cream. Oil a large rectangular pan on the bottom and sides. Add bell peppers, cilantro and onion then pour the egg mixture over. Sprinkle the shredded cheeses on top and cover the pan with foil.
» Place the pan on the barbecue on indirect heat (or in the oven) and cook until you can jiggle the pan and nothing moves. Cool and cut into squares using a spatula.
» To make the sandwich, toast each slice of bread on one side. Spread the bottom half with Dijonnaise, add a lettuce leaf, a piece of bacon and a thin slice of omelet. Lightly season. Add the other slice of toasted bread, cut in half and serve with the sausage and some salsa if you like.

* *

CHAPTER 2

83

LAMB AND PORK

SLOW SMOKED PORK RIBS

Serves 6

* *

The type of barbecue you have will determine the method of cooking. If you have a smoker and you can regulate the temperature to keep it steadily below 170°F, you can cool smoke the ribs for up to 3 hours. That's what I do. On most outdoor grills, cooking times will be much less, because the meat is closer to the heat source. For this reason, an offset smoker tends to work better. No matter what you cook on, the exact time will depend on how thick the ribs are, how steady you have kept the temperature and how close to the heat source the ribs are. Use to the traditional Texas 3, 2, 1 method (page 21). This works on my barbecue but may not work on some. For this recipe, you will need some fruitwood for smoking.

INGREDIENTS

2 pork rib racks, St Louis style
4 fl oz (125 ml) extra virgin olive oil
1 batch Pork Rib Rub (page 192)
1 batch Quick Barbecue Sauce (page 154)

Barbecue Sauce Glaze
1 tablespoon honey
1 tablespoon brown sugar
4 fl oz (125 ml) water
2 fl oz (60 ml) commercial barbecue sauce

METHOD

» Allow the ribs to come to room temperature. Trim the ribs and remove the silverskin.
» Rub oil over the rib racks then rub in the Basic Pork Rib Rub. Set aside for at least 1–2 hours.
» Preheat your barbecue to medium high, 400°F (200°C) with a good bed of coals.
» Get the smoke going from some fruitwood before you put the ribs in the smoker. When the ribs are at room temperature, place inside the smoker, bone side down. Keep the temperature steady in the firebox area at below 170° F (77° C) to cool smoke the ribs for up to 3 hours.
» When they are sufficiently colored and smoked, coat with the barbecue sauce and wrap them tightly in foil.
» Cook at 220°–250°F (105°–130°C) for about 2 hours checking after the first 1¼ hours how things are going as cooking times can vary.
» Test the meat with a visual bend test—check if the meat cracks after being picked up and bent at one end. Meat thermometers are not much good on ribs as they are too thin.
» Unwrap the ribs. Mix the barbecue sauce glaze ingredients together and brush over the ribs.
» Keep the wrap slightly open and cook for a further 30 minutes to 1 hour. The internal temperature should be around 185° F (90° C) When the glaze looks a bit shiny, the ribs are done.
» Serve with your favorite salad or slaw.

NOTE This goes well with dill pickles and any bean dish of choice. Make sure you don't overcook— total cooking time should be 5–6 hours for custom-cut St Louis style ribs or 3–4 for baby backs.

* *

Chapter 3

CHICKEN

BARBECUED CHICKEN

Serves 5

A good barbecue chicken rub usually has salt, pepper, sage, thyme and/or bay leaves. You can use almost any good quality rub recipe accompanied with a barbecue sauce to create an adequate rub.

INGREDIENTS

1 large chicken (3 lb/1½ kg)
extra virgin olive oil, for cooking
Barbecue Chicken Rub (page 194)
8 oz (250 g) breadcrumbs
1 large egg, lightly beaten
2 teaspoons garlic
1 teaspoon onion salt

black pepper, to taste
2 small apples, roughly chopped
2 stalks celery, roughly chopped
1 medium white onion, roughly chopped
2 large carrots, roughly chopped
6 oz (200 ml) chicken stock

METHOD

» Preheat barbecue to 325–350ºF (170–180ºC).
» Rub the chicken thoroughly with olive oil then rub in the chicken rub putting some under the skin. Place in an airtight bag in the refrigerator for at least 2 hours or overnight if possible.
» Remove about 20 minutes before cooking to bring the chicken to room temperature.
» To make stuffing, combine breadcrumbs, egg, garlic, onion salt and pepper in a bowl. Mix thoroughly and stuff the chicken. Alternatively, use your own favorite recipe or buy prepared stuffing.
» Place apple, celery, onions and carrots in one layer on a foil pan. Place the chicken, breast up, on the vegetable/fruit layer. Pour over with chicken stock.
» Cover the top of the tray with the foil and cook the chicken in a covered barbecue for about 1¼–1¾ hours, depending on weight—allow 1 hour per 1 lb (500 g).
» After 1 hour, use a meat thermometer to check the chicken at the meatiest part of the breast between the bones. The chicken is ready when it reads an internal temperature of 165–175°F (75–80ºC) on the breast and 185ºF (84ºC) on the thigh. You can remove the chicken when the temperature is 10ºF (5ºC) shy of the thigh mark.
» Uncover the chicken and brush with some barbecue sauce directly onto the skin to get that 'barbecue chicken taste'. Put chicken back on a high indirect heat, 450˚F (230˚C) for a few minutes to get a crispy skin (or grill the chicken on direct heat for a few minutes for the same result). If using an oven, turn the broiler (grill) to high and place the chicken uncovered about 6 inch (15 cm) from the direct heat source. This will not take long, so don't overcook it. Remove the chicken and rest for 7–8 minutes.
» Serve on a platter with the pan juices and roasted vegetables such as mushrooms, potatoes and carrots.

NOTE A stuffed chicken takes a bit longer to cook than one that is not stuffed.

BAKED CHICKEN FINGERS

Serves 6

* *

Kids love to munch on these, and so does just about everyone else. They are so popular, you'll need to cook some extras for lunch boxes.

INGREDIENTS

1 pint (600 ml) milk

2 eggs, beaten

olive oil cooking spray

6 medium chicken breasts (6 oz/200 g each)

1 lb (500 g) all-purpose (plain) flour

2 tablespoons onion salt

2 tablespoons garlic salt

1 teaspoon freshly ground black pepper

METHOD

» Heat barbecue or oven to 450°F (220ºC).

» Mix the milk and eggs together.

» Line a flat tray with foil and spray with cooking oil. Place chicken in a shallow dish with the egg mixture.

» Mix the flour, onion salt, garlic salt and pepper in a large bowl or square container.

» Place the egg/milk-soaked chicken in the seasoned flour and coat on all sides.

» Cook the coated chicken for 15–20 minutes on a covered barbecue (or oven), turning once, until chicken is no longer pink in the center and the coating is golden brown.

» Remove from heat, pat chicken with paper towels and drain on a wire rack. Rest the chicken for 2–3 minutes.

» Serve with a dipping sauce of your choice.

NOTE Texan White Gravy (page 172) goes well with these.

* *

CHICKEN BREAST WITH PINEAPPLE AND ONIONS

Serves 4

* *

This is a simple and easy way to cook chicken. The combination of pineapple and onions with the chicken make this a tasty treat.

INGREDIENTS

2 tablespoons extra virgin olive oil

4 chicken breasts, butterflied (tenderized), or 4 thighs, bone removed and butterflied

½ teaspoon sea salt

1 teaspoon freshly ground black pepper

1 large white onion, cut in large rings

1 pineapple, cut in strips

2 tablespoons cilantro (coriander) fresh-chopped

1 lime, juiced

salsa of choice (pages 169–172)

cooked white rice (Jasmine), to serve

METHOD

» Preheat barbecue to medium-high heat—400°F (200°C) for grilling (over hot coals).

» Oil the entire surface on both sides of the butterflied chicken, then place on a flat pan and season with salt and pepper.

» Brush grill with oil then brush onion and pineapple with oil. Cook on barbecue until lightly charred. Set aside. When cool, roughly chop and mix together in a bowl. Add cilantro and lime juice.

» Place chicken on the hot grill and cook for 6–8 minutes. If using thighs, allow 9–12 minutes. Remove when chicken is golden-brown all over and cooked through.

» Directly after cooking, place chicken on a platter. Spoon over the pineapple and onion, add the salsa and serve with fragrant white rice.

NOTE Ask your butcher to butterfly chicken or do it yourself. Butterflied (tenderized) chicken makes it easier to cook evenly. Remember, the breast cooks faster than the thigh, making it harder to keep moist.

* *

LIME CHICKEN

Serves 4

* *

Here is another relatively simple way to create a very pleasing chicken dish.

INGREDIENTS

6 oz (200 g) skinless, boneless chicken breast cut into
  ½ inch (1 cm) thin pieces
extra virgin olive oil cooking spray
¼ teaspoon salt

Marinade

2 tablespoons cilantro (coriander), minced
2 limes, juiced
1½ tablespoons avocado oil
salt, to taste

Salsa

2 tomatoes, chopped
2 white onions, finely chopped
1 lime, juiced
1 avocado, peeled and diced
salt and pepper, to taste

METHOD

» Place the chicken pieces into a sealable plastic bag or container with an airtight lid.
» Prepare the marinade by putting all the ingredients in a large bowl, toss and let stand for 3 minutes.
» Add the marinade to the chicken pieces and allow to marinate for at least 2–3 hours then remove chicken from marinade. Discard marinade. Sprinkle chicken evenly with about ¼ teaspoon salt.
» Preheat your barbecue grill to medium high, 400°F (200°C).
» Coat the pan with oil and heat on the barbecue.
» Add chicken to pan and cook for 5–6 minutes on each side or until done.
» To prepare salsa, combine the ingredients in a medium bowl. Add the avocado at the last minute to keep it from discoloring. Combine gently and serve with (or over) the pan-grilled chicken.

NOTE If you can't get avocado oil, use any high-quality cooking oil.

* *

BUFFALO WINGS

Serves 8

* *

Didn't you always wonder why these were called buffalo wings? That's where they were originally cooked—in Buffalo. These need to cook *slowly* with little or no sizzle for the best results.

INGREDIENTS

2 lb (1 kg) chicken wings
2 tablespoons extra virgin olive oil
salt, to taste

Buffalo Barbecue Sauce
4 oz (125 g) unsalted butter
12 tablespoons hot sauce (Tabasco)

2 teaspoons Worcestershire sauce
1 teaspoon salt
1 teaspoon sugar
1 teaspoon garlic powder
1 teaspoon freshly ground black pepper
1 teaspoon cayenne pepper

METHOD

» Using a paring knife or poultry shears, cut off the wing tips and either discard (or freeze for your own chicken stock later).
» Use the knife or shears to separate the wing drums from the flats (the mid-joint wings).
» Toss the flats with the oil and salt, and arrange in one layer in a disposable aluminum foil pan.
» To make the sauce, add all the ingredients to a small saucepan and heat until the butter melts. Do not allow to boil. Once melted, remove from heat and whisk to combine all the ingredients. Set aside. If the sauce thickens, whisk again over low heat before using.
» Heat barbecue to low, 180ºF (82ºC). Place pan over indirect heat. If you are using charcoal or wood on a smaller barbecue, set your fire on one side of the grill and arrange the tray with wings on the other side. Cook on barbecue with the cover down for 30 minutes.
» Turn the wings and brush with the barbecue sauce. Close the barbecue lid again and cook for another 30 minutes.
» Repeat the process, brushing with the sauce, until the wings are done to your liking, now brushing every 15 minutes or so—make sure you leave some sauce for serving. If you want crispy skin, place on a flat, well-oiled barbecue grill over direct hot heat for a few minutes on each side. In you are using an oven, do this under the broiler (grill). Remove from heat and rest for 2–3 minutes.
» Toss with the leftover sauce and serve.

NOTE These can also be chicken fried and tossed in the hot sauce. The original flavor has Tabasco and cayenne pepper, but you can use something different, but don't call them buffalo wings if they don't have the cayenne pepper and hot sauce.

* *

CHICKEN AND MUSHROOM PATTIES

Makes 6

* *

If you like to eat chicken and mushrooms, here is a great way to get them together on the plate.

INGREDIENTS

16 oz (500 g) chicken, ground

8 oz (250 g) mushrooms, diced

2 scallions (spring onions), chopped

1 carrot, peeled and grated

1 tablespoon chili powder

¾ teaspoon salt

¼ teaspoon cumin powder

½ teaspoon freshly ground black pepper

extra virgin olive oil

mashed potatoes, to serve

salad of choice, to serve

METHOD

» Combine chicken, mushrooms, scallions, carrot, chili powder, salt, cumin and ground black pepper. Mix thoroughly.

» Form palm-sized burgers, leaving the center pressed down a little.

» Preheat barbecue to medium high, 400°F (200°C.)

» Coat a cast-iron frypan (skillet) with cooking oil and heat on the barbecue until the oil becomes very hot. Cook the patties for about 4–6 minutes on each side or until cooked through. Alternatively, cook them directly on a flat grill barbecue plate on direct, medium-high heat. Remove from heat, pat with a paper towel and set on a wire rack. Rest for 1–2 minutes.

» Serve with mashed potatoes and a fresh salad.

NOTE The chicken patties also make a great alternative to the chicken breast used in Chicken Burgers (page 103).

* *

CHICKEN GIZZARDS

Serves 4

* *

Kids in particular have fun with these (also called chicken hearts) and they really do taste amazing. Makes a good appetizer with Murphy's Ranch Dressing (page 173) used as a dip.

INGREDIENTS

1 lb (500 g) chicken gizzards or 1 lb (500 g) chicken hearts
6 fl oz (200 ml) milk
2 large eggs, beaten
4 pints (2 L) extra virgin olive oil, for frying

Coating
12 oz (375 g) flour
1½ teaspoons salt
4 oz (125 g) bread crumbs
1 teaspoon garlic powder
1 teaspoon freshly ground black pepper
1 teaspoon paprika

METHOD

» Clean the gizzards, removing any foreign matter. Wash thoroughly and place in a bowl of milk mixed with eggs. Mix the coating ingredients together. Place the gizzards in the flour mixture and coat evenly.
» Preheat your barbecue grill to medium high, 400˚F (200˚C).
» Add the oil to a frypan or Dutch oven and heat on the barbecue then add the coated gizzards to the heated oil and fry on all sides until golden brown. Do not overcook as these will become very tough and they are a bit chewy anyway.
» Pat excess oil off with a paper towel and rest on a wire rack. Allow to rest for 2–3 minutes.
» Serve warm with your choice of sauce.

NOTE Mayonnaise, mustard or Murphy's Ranch Dressing (page 173) all go well with these or any of the sauces (pages 154–166).

* *

CHICKEN RIBS

Serves 6

* *

These are a real crowd pleaser. I serve these sometimes with beef short ribs and pork ribs as an appetizer. It is always funny to hear people say, "Wow! I didn't even know chickens had ribs!" Huh? Warning: If you take these to a party, there may be a brawl over who gets to eat the most. Cook some extras for the police when they arrive.

INGREDIENTS

30 chicken ribs
1 pt (500 ml) buttermilk
2 large eggs, lightly beaten
4 pt (2 L) extra virgin olive oil
1 lb (500 g) all-purpose (plain) flour

2 tablespoons garlic powder
2 tablespoons onion powder
1–2 tablespoons chili powder, optional
1 teaspoon cayenne pepper
salt and freshly ground pepper, to taste

METHOD

» Trim off the excess fat and skin from the ribs. Wash and pat dry.
» In a bowl, mix together the milk and eggs. Add the chicken, cover and leave in the refrigerator for about 1 hour.
» Preheat the barbecue to 300°F (175°C).
» Mix all the dry ingredients in a large bowl or square container.
» Put a cast-iron frypan on the hot barbecue. Add 1 inch (3 cm) of the oil. The oil is hot enough when you drop in a small amount of flour and it immediately starts to bubble. If the chicken pieces are small, you can use a higher heat.
» Place the buttermilk-soaked chicken in the dry mix and coat on all sides with the seasoned flour, then immediately place in the hot pan. Fry for 3–4 minutes on each side, or until it turns golden brown. If you use a deep fryer, it takes about 3–3½ minutes on 350°F (180°C).
» Remove the chicken and pat dry gently with paper towels then drain on a wire rack. Rest for 3–4 minutes.
» Serve with your favorite condiments.

NOTE Try these with Texan White Gravy (page 172), Murphy's Ranch Dressing (page 173) or Honey Mustard Sauce (page 162). You will have to buy these chicken ribs at a specialty chicken shop. Get them as fresh as you can. Find out when they come in off the truck and get them the same day.

* *

CHICKEN SALAD ROLL

Serves 6-8

* *

This is not a piece of chicken breast with some lettuce on a bun. This is a proper salad made with chicken and it tastes wonderful.

INGREDIENTS

3 lb (1½ kg) chicken breast, cooked

2 large celery stalks, finely sliced

¼ large red onion, sliced

4 scallions (spring onions), sliced

1 large jalapeño, seeds removed and diced

12 oz (375 g) craisins (dried sweetened cranberries)

1 tablespoon red hot sauce

4 oz (125 g) pecans, toasted and chopped, optional

½ bunch parsley, chopped

16 oz (500 g) mayonnaise

½ lemon, juiced

salt and freshly ground black pepper

6–8 bread rolls (or bread), to serve

METHOD

» Shred the chicken and cut into bite-sized pieces.

» Combine chicken with celery, onion, scallions, jalapeño, craisins, sauce, pecans, parsley and mayonnaise in a large mixing bowl. Add lemon juice to taste. Season with salt and pepper.

» Slice bread rolls in half but not all the way through. Add the mixture to each roll and serve.

NOTE You can add tomatoes, shredded carrots, lettuce, dill
or other salad vegetables if you like.

* *

CHICKEN BURGERS

Makes 4

* *

Did someone say chicken burgers? If you feel like a hamburger without the beef, or you just like chicken, then you'll love these burgers.

INGREDIENTS

4 chicken breast pieces (skinless)
1 pint (500 ml) milk
2 large eggs, beaten
1 lb (500 g) all-purpose (plain) flour
1 teaspoon chili flakes
2 tablespoons paprika
½ teaspoon onion salt
1 teaspoon garlic salt
½ teaspoon chicken salt

1 teaspoon freshly ground black pepper
4 oz (125 g) breadcrumbs
extra virgin olive oil
4 hamburger buns
1–2 tomatoes, sliced
4 iceburg lettuce slices or rocket
1 red onion, finely sliced
3–4 dill pickles

METHOD

» Cover the chicken breast with clear wrap and tenderize (by hitting with a mallet) until it is an even thickness. Cut or trim to the size of a burger pattie.
» Mix egg and milk together and place the chicken patties in the mixture. Allow the chicken to sit in the mixture for at least 30 minutes in the refrigerator.
» While the chicken is marinating, place the flour, herbs, spices and breadcrumbs in a shallow dish and mix together.
» Remove chicken from the refrigerator, drain off any excess milk/egg mixture and coat the chicken evenly with your flour mixture.
» Place a frypan (skillet) or Dutch oven directly on the barbecue grill and heat oil. The oil should half fill the pan.
» Cook the chicken until golden brown and crispy on each side. Drain on a wire rack and pat with paper towels. Salt lightly while these are still warm. Rest for 2–3 minutes.
» Serve each chicken piece on a toasted hamburger bun with tomato, rocket or lettuce, red onion, dill pickle and cheese.

NOTE The same old familiar condiments go well with chicken burgers:
barbecue sauce, ketchup, mayonnaise and mustards.

* *

CILANTRO LIME CHICKEN

Serves 4

* *

This chicken dish is a light and refreshing, probably more suitable for a lunch or a light dinner.

INGREDIENTS

4 x 6 oz (200 g) skinless chicken breast halves
salt, to taste
cooking oil spray

Marinade

2 tablespoons cilantro (coriander), freshly minced
2½ tablespoons fresh lime juice
1½ tablespoons extra virgin olive oil

Salsa

½ lb (250 g) tomatoes, chopped
2 tablespoons onion, finely chopped
1 avocado, peeled and chopped
2 teaspoons fresh lime juice
salt and freshly ground black pepper, to taste

METHOD

» Cover the chicken breast with clear wrap and tenderize (by hitting with a mallet) until it is an even thickness.
» Combine marinade ingredients in a large bowl then add the chicken. Toss and let stand for 30 minutes or until the chicken reaches room temperature.
» Remove chicken from marinade. Discard marinade. Sprinkle chicken evenly with salt.
» Heat barbecue grill plate to medium high, 400°F (200°C).
» Place chicken over direct heat on the barbecue grill (or in a oiled frypan on the stove top).
» Cook 4–6 minutes on each side (depending on thickness), or until done.
» Allow to rest for 4–5 minutes on a wire rack.
» To make the salsa, combine all ingredients. Season with salt and pepper to taste.
» Serve chicken with the salsa spooned on top.

NOTE For something different, serve with Pico de Gallo (page 127) or
any other salsa (pages 169–172).

* *

KING RANCH CHICKEN

Serves 6

* *

This is an all-time favorite casserole dish. What makes this a Texan casserole is the spices used. Jalapeño peppers have a bit of a kick. This is a slightly spicy, cheesy mixture of tomatoes, corn tortillas, chicken, cream and peppers. What a great dish to eat on a winter's night—or any night really.

INGREDIENTS

5 lb (2 kg) whole chicken
2 celery stalks, cut into 3 pieces each
2 medium carrots, cut into 3 pieces each
2 small jalapeños, deseeded
3 teaspoons salt
2 tablespoons butter
1 medium onion, chopped
1 medium green bell pepper (capsicum), diced
1 medium red bell pepper (capsicum), diced
1 garlic clove, pressed

8 fl oz (250 ml) canned cream of mushroom soup
8 fl oz (250 ml) canned cream of chicken soup
16 fl oz (500 ml) canned diced tomatoes, drained
1 teaspoon dried oregano
1 teaspoon ground cumin
1 teaspoon Mexican-style chili powder
16 oz (500 g) tasty cheddar cheese, grated
12 x 6 inch (15 cm) fajita-sized corn tortillas, cut into
   ½ inch (1 cm) strips
salt and pepper, to taste

METHOD

» Rinse chicken then place the chicken, celery, carrots, jalapeños and salt in a large Dutch oven with water to cover. Bring to the boil over medium-high heat then reduce to low. Cover and simmer for 50 minutes to 1 hour or until chicken is cooked. Remove from heat.

» Remove chicken from broth reserving ¾ cup cooking liquid (stock). Strain remaining cooking liquid, and reserve for another use.

» Cool the chicken for 30 minutes then remove the skin and bones and discard. Shred the chicken meat into bite-sized pieces.

» Preheat oven to 350°F (180ºC).

» Melt butter in a large frypan on the stove top over medium-high heat. Add onion and sauté for 6–7 minutes, or until translucent.

» Add bell peppers and garlic, then sauté for 3–4 minutes. Stir in reserved ¾ cup cooking liquid, mushroom soup, chicken soup, tomatoes, oregano, cumin and chili powder. Cook, stirring occasionally, for about 8 minutes.

» Preheat barbecue to 350°F (180ºC).

» Layer half of the chicken meat in a lightly-greased 9 x 13 inch (23 x 33 cm) baking dish. Top with half of the soup mixture and half of the cheese. Cover with half of the corn tortilla strips. Repeat the layering again. Top with the remaining cheese.

» Cover the baking dish and place on a covered barbecue. Bake for 50 minutes to 1 hour, or until bubbly.

» Let stand for 10 minutes before serving.

* *

SOUTHERN FRIED CHICKEN

Serves 4

· ·

This is the real deal that is served up throughout the south of the US. It's a healthier version of takeaway chicken and tastes better too. It will be easier with a heavy-bottomed cast-iron frypan or Dutch oven or even a deep fryer. I use a Dutch oven on the barbecue and a deep fryer if cooking in the kitchen.

INGREDIENTS

1 medium chicken, cut into 8 pieces, skin removed (or leave it on for extra crisp)

4 pt (2 L) buttermilk

3 large eggs, beaten

4 pt (2 L) extra virgin olive oil for cooking

Flour and Spice Mix

1 lb (½ kg) all-purpose (plain) flour

2 tablespoons garlic powder

2 tablespoons onion powder

1 teaspoon cumin powder

2 tablespoons chili powder

1 teaspoon cayenne pepper

1 teaspoon salt

1 teaspoon fresh ground black pepper

4 oz (125 g) breadcrumbs, crumbled cornflakes or crushed crackers (optional)

METHOD

» Whisk together the buttermilk and eggs in a large bowl. Place chicken pieces in the buttermilk mixture, cover and place in the refrigerator for 1 hour.

» Remove from the refrigerator and allow chicken to come to room temperature. Mix all the dry ingredients in a large bowl or square container. You might need to add more flour and spices as you start to use up the ingredients.

» Place the buttermilk-soaked chicken in the dry mix and coat on all sides. Place chicken on a clean tray.

» Preheat a cast-iron frypan with 1 inch (3 cm) of oil to 300ºF (175ºC) or heat the oil to the point that, when you drop in a small amount of flour, it immediately starts to bubble. If chicken pieces are smaller, use a higher heat.

» Fry chicken in the pan for about 12 minutes or 6 minutes on each side. If using a deep fryer check with an internal temperature gauge, 165ºF (74ºC) for the breast pieces and 185ºF (83ºC) for the thigh. The size of the pieces dictates the cooking temperature and time, lower heat and longer times for larger pieces.

» When pieces are golden brown and cooked properly, rest on a wire rack to make sure the chicken stays crispy.

» Allow chicken to rest for 5–7 minutes before serving.

NOTE This goes very well with Texan White Gravy (page 172). If you are using pan juices to make the gravy, make sure you drain most of the oil from the pan. Be sure the individual pieces are not too large as the result can be overcooked on the outside and not cooked enough in the middle.

· ·

CHICKEN SOUP

Serves 6

* *

Want to get well soon? Have some chicken soup. This stuff will cure whatever ails you. It has been proven that chicken soup actually has some medicinal value. Try this recipe even if you're not sick.

INGREDIENTS

6 chicken thighs, bones in

2 tablespoons butter

½ lb (250 g) onions, diced

½ lb (250 g) celery, diced

½ lb (250 g) carrots, diced

4 sprigs thyme

1 teaspoon garlic, minced

2 jalapeño peppers, seeded and diced

1½ teaspoons salt

½ teaspoons cumin, ground

1 tablespoon tomato paste

3 pt (1.5 L) water or chicken stock

4 tablespoons cilantro (coriander), chopped

2 teaspoons fresh lime juice

1 avocado, peeled, seeded and chopped, for garnish

extra virgin olive oil, for cooking

METHOD

» In a large, heavy pot, heat the butter on medium-high heat. Brown the chicken thighs on all sides and add some salt.

» Add the onions, celery, carrots, thyme, garlic, jalapeño peppers, salt, cumin and cook for 5 minutes.

» Add the tomato paste and cook, stirring, for 1 minute.

» Add the water/chicken stock. Bring to a boil, lower heat and simmer for 30 minutes.

» Add the cilantro and lime juice, and stir well.

» Remove the chicken, allow to cool and take out the bones. Discard the bones.

» Cut the chicken into bite-sized pieces and put back into the pot. Stir and simmer for a few more minutes.

» Remove from the heat and cover to keep warm. Serve the soup into 6 serving bowls.

» Garnish each serving with the avocado pieces.

NOTE As a variation, you can make the chicken stock beforehand. Brown the chicken, boil it and remove the skin and bones. Leave the stock to cool and then put it in the refrigerator. The fat will rise to the top and solidify. This is an effective technique to remove some of the fat from the process.

* *

CHICKEN ENCHILADAS

Serves 6

* *

Enchiladas originated in Mexico, where the practice of rolling tortillas around other food dates back to at least Mayan times. This is an easy version that is so good you could eat them off the bottom of your boot, although I don't recommend that you do.

INGREDIENTS
12 fl oz (375 ml) canned creamy chicken soup
8 oz (250 g) sour cream
8 fl oz (250 ml) chicken stock
1 medium onion, diced
3 jalapeños, seeds removed and diced
1 medium chicken, boiled, de-boned and diced

8 oz (250 g) grated cheese
10 corn or flour tortillas
1 red chili, seeds removed and thinly cut, for garnish
Pico de Gallo (page 127), to serve
corn chips, to serve

METHOD
» Preheat barbecue or oven to 350°F (175°C).
» Put the chicken soup in a saucepan and heat slowly while stirring. Add sour cream and chicken stock.
» In a frypan, sauté the onion and jalapeños and add, with the diced chicken, to the chicken soup. Add half the cheese to form a thick, creamy consistency. Allow to cool slightly.
» Put some of the mix on each tortilla, roll the tortillas up and place in an ovenproof dish. Pour the remaining mix over the top of the tortillas and sprinkle with cheese on top. Cover with foil.
» Place on a covered barbecue on indirect heat (or in the oven) for 20 minutes. Uncover, garnish with chili slices and a bit more cheese and place under the grill for 5–10 minutes, or until it starts to get some good color.
» Serve with Pico de Gallo or any other salsa (pages 169–172) that you like and corn chips.

NOTE Enchiladas can be filled with meat, cheese, beans, potatoes, vegetables, seafood or combinations of just about anything really.

* *

110   **CHAPTER 3**

CHICKEN WRAPS

Serves 6

* *

This dish is more of a roulade ('roll' in French) than a wrap. Traditionally, it uses boneless chicken breasts, stuffed to the gills with cheeses, vegetables, and other meats.

INGREDIENTS

6 slices ham, off the bone

6 slices tasty cheese

6 slices liverwurst

1 small red onion, diced

6 chicken breasts halved, boned, skinned and
   tenderized (save the skin)

2 tablespoons butter

extra virgin olive oil, for cooking

2 fl oz (60 ml) white wine or juice of 2 lemons

2 tablespoons soy sauce

1 teaspoon black pepper

1 small red onion, diced

salt and freshly ground black pepper, to taste

sauce or condiments of choice, to serve

METHOD

» Lay out a slice of ham, then layer the cheese and the liverwurst and roll together.

» Cut the chicken breast in a half (not all the way through. Put the ham bundle *inside* the chicken breast, close and wrap with a piece of chicken skin brushed with butter. Tie with string so the wrap holds its shape. Repeat until you have made all the wraps.

» Preheat the barbecue to 350ºF (175ºC).

» Grease a cooking dish (or foil pan) with butter and place the wraps in the dish. Add the wine, soy sauce, black pepper and diced onion. Cover the dish and place on the barbecue over indirect heat. Cook for 35–45 minutes.

» Remove the cover. Remove the wraps from the dish, brush with oil, and place on a well-oiled hot plate until the desired golden color and crispy skin is achieved—or you can place them under a broiler (grill) for a few minutes. Season with salt and pepper. Allow to rest for 2–4 minutes.

» Serve with your choice of condiments or sauces such as barbecue, ketchup, mayonnaise or mustard.

NOTE You can add other types of cheese, vegetables and other meats to
create your own wrap/roulade inventions.

* *

HALVED QUAIL

Serves 6

- -

I know that this isn't chicken, but I kinda snuck this one in anyway because it's so good. As good as quail is to eat, this is the best yet. In some parts of the world, quail hunting and farming is a huge industry. Here's one good reason for that.

INGREDIENTS

3 whole quails
2 large eggs
1 pt (500 ml) skim milk
extra virgin olive oil, for cooking
Murphy's Ranch Dressing (page 173)
Texan White Gravy (page 172)

Flour Mix
1 lb (500g) all-purpose (plain) flour
2 tablespoons garlic salt
2 tablespoons onion salt
1 tablespoon salt
1½ teaspoon freshly ground black pepper

METHOD

» Using a pair of scissors, cut along the backbone and breast of the quails to cut the birds in half down the middle.
» Mix the egg and milk and place the quail halves in the mixture for at least 1 hour.
» Mix the flour ingredients together in a plastic container with lid, large enough to put one quail half in for coating.
» Remove the quail halves from the milk and place one at a time in the container. With the lid on, shake to coat. Repeat until all six quail halves are coated.
» Allow quails to rest at room temperature for 10–20 minutes before cooking. You may have to apply a little more dry mix after they rest.
» Preheat the barbecue and place a Dutch oven with 2 inch (5 cm) of oil on the hot barbecue. Test oil temperature by dropping some flour into the oil. If the oil bubbles, it's ready.
» Fry the quails until they are lightly golden brown on each side. Be gentle—you only need to turn them once. If using a deep fryer, set to 320°F (160°C). Deep fry for 3–4 minutes or until lightly golden brown.
» Drain on wire racks and pat with paper towels. Salt lightly while still hot then allow to rest for 3–5 minutes.
» Serve with Murphy's Ranch Dressing, Texan White Gravy or your favorite sauce.

NOTE Use only the quail thighs and legs as an appetizer. Some quails are much larger than others. This recipe is for a smaller variety of quail but will work for larger birds, but the cooking times will be different.

- -

COWBOY CHICKEN AND RICE CASSEROLE

Serves 6

A cowboy chicken can be easily identified by his boots, hat and his horse (only cowboy chickens ride horses). This is the perfect dish to make over the weekend, assembled Monday morning before work and cooked for a quick 30-minute heat-through for Monday evening.

INGREDIENTS

2 tablespoons butter
2 scallions (spring onions), diced
2 medium onions, finely chopped
1 garlic clove, minced
2 celery stalks, diced
1 small packet white rice
1 whole barbecued chicken (page 89), deboned and chopped into bite-size pieces
8 oz (250 g) fresh mushrooms, chopped

16 fl oz (500 ml) chicken stock
4 fl oz (125 ml) mayonnaise
1 teaspoon Worcestershire sauce
1 teaspoon Tabasco sauce
12 green beans, washed and cut into 1 inch (2½ cm) lengths
1 can chicken soup or celery soup
4 oz (125 g) cheese, grated

METHOD

» Add butter to a frypan and sauté scallions, onions, garlic and celery over a medium-low heat.
» Boil the white rice until cooked (drain off the water) and place in a large bowl. Add and mix all the other ingredients except for the cheese.
» Place in a buttered or lightly-oiled casserole dish for oven or an oiled tin pan for barbecue.
» Sprinkle cheese on top then cook at 350ºF or (175ºC) for 30 minutes.
» Serve with your favorite salad.

Chapter 4

SIDE DISHES

BAKED BEANS WITH CHORIZO AND BACON

Serves 6

* *

I was cooking chorizo way before chorizo was cool. Let's put in some beans which is kind of like bacon—it makes everything taste great. OK, let's put some bacon in there too.

INGREDIENTS

4 slices streaky bacon

2 chorizo sausages

1 small onion, diced

1 jalapeño, seeds removed and diced

2 cans x 12 oz (375 g) baked beans

2 oz (120 ml) barbecue sauce

2 oz (120 g) brown sugar or ketchup

1 teaspoon dry mustard

1 teaspoon Dijon mustard

METHOD

» Fry the bacon on a barbecue hotplate or in a frypan until they are crispy. Cool then cut or crumble into small pieces.

» Fry the chorizos on the barbecue hotplate. Slice in half as they cook to get a thorough cook on all sides. Remove, cool then dice the sausages.

» Fry the onion and diced jalapeño in a Dutch oven or large pot. Add bacon, chorizo and baked beans, barbecue sauce, brown sugar and mustards.

» Cover with a lid and simmer for 20–30 minutes.

» Serve with Barbecued Pork Chops (page 75) or Texas Style Brisket (page 54).

* *

BARBECUED BUTTERNUT SQUASH

Serves 6

* *

What is sexier than pumpkin on the barbecue? OK, just about everything. Anyway, it has some curves and it is great to throw a vegetable on a barbecue grill.

INGREDIENTS

1 large butternut squash, cut length ways into 1 inch
  (3 cm) thick strips
2–3 tablespoons extra virgin olive oil
1½ teaspoons salt

1½ teaspoons pepper
½ teaspoon brown sugar
½ teaspoon nutmeg

METHOD

» Mix olive oil, salt, pepper, brown sugar and nutmeg. Coat both sides of pumpkin strips 3/4 of the spice mix.
» Cook on a barbecue grill or hot plate for 10–12 minutes on each side, or until cooked through. Sprinkle the rest of the spice mix over the pumpkin.
» Serve.

* *

CHICHARONNES

Serves 4

* *

Despite my wife's objections, I fed these by the handful to my kids when they were little and they still survived. This is a tasty snack, or great appetizer. You eat one and you can't stop.

INGREDIENTS
12 oz (375 ml) extra virgin olive oil
16 oz (500 g) uncooked boneless pork butt, roast or
  pork belly, skin removed, cut into 3/4 inch (1½ cm)
  cubes (½ meat, ½ fat)
salt, to taste

METHOD
» Preheat your barbecue to medium-high heat, 400°F (200°C).
» Put oil into a large frying pan and heat on the barbecue. Test the readiness of the oil by dropping in a small piece of pork. If it sizzles instantly, it is ready.
» Add pork pieces and fry evenly all over for about 5–7 minutes. Using tongs, stir pork around in the hot pan for about 2 more minutes or until you see a nice golden caramelized color on the pork.
» After cooking, drain on paper towels then place in a tea towel and squeeze out the oil.
» Place pork in a large bowl. Add salt.
» Serve warm.

NOTE I have seen other ways to make chicharonnes. This was how I was taught and it works for me. They can also be cooked in a deep fryer.

* *

EASY TEXAN CAVIAR

Serves 6-8

* *

Caviar is from fish, right? But there is none in this dish. If you had a choice between the black fish eggs and this, I think you would eat more of this. It tastes better and costs a lot less.

INGREDIENTS

12 oz (375 ml) Black-eyed Pea Soup (page 144)

12 oz (375 ml) can black beans, drained

16 oz (500 g) corn, fresh or frozen

1 small red onion, minced

1 small green bell pepper (capsicum), diced

1 small red bell pepper (capsicum), diced

1 jalapeño, seeds removed, finely chopped

3 cloves garlic, minced

¼ bunch cilantro (coriander), finely chopped

3 green onions, sliced, stalks and all

4 tablespoons extra virgin olive oil

2 tablespoons red wine vinegar

2 teaspoons salt

1 lime, juiced

METHOD

» Add all ingredients to a large bowl and toss to combine.

» Cover and refrigerate.

» Serve with barbecued burgers, sandwiches, or with any fish or meat dish.

NOTE This is very easy to make because you've already made
your Black-eyed Pea Soup (page 144).

* *

CUCUMBER SALAD

Serves 6

* *

Why cucumber salad? It keeps you hydrated. It fights heat, both inside and out. It flushes out toxins. It lavishes you with vitamins. It is full of skin-friendly minerals—magnesium, potassium and silicon. It aids weight loss. It revives the eyes.

OK, let's just eat cucumbers and nothing else.

INGREDIENTS

2 cucumbers, peeled and cut into thin slices
¼ white onion, finely sliced
1 teaspoon salt

8 fl oz (250 ml) Murphy's Ranch Dressing
  (page 173)

METHOD

» Chill both cucumbers and dressing first.
» Combine ingredients and serve immediately.

NOTE The ranch dressing makes this dish but you can make a variation of this simple salad using yogurt, sour cream or mayonnaise.

* *

PICO DE GALLO

Serves 6

* *

This has been a side dish for way over a hundred years in Mexican cuisine. Pico de Gallo literally means rooster's beak. It's also called salsa fresca because it is such a fresh-tasting salad. This not only looks great, it tastes great and makes everything else taste better.

WARNING: You can get addicted to this.

INGREDIENTS

3 medium, firm tomatoes, diced
3 jalapeños, seeds removed and diced
1 medium red onion, diced
½ bunch cilantro (coriander), finely chopped

1 scallion (spring onion) stalk and all, diced
1 lime, juiced, to taste
salt and pepper, to taste

METHOD

» In a bowl, mix together tomatoes, jalapeños, red onion, cilantro and scallion. Add lime juice. Season with salt and pepper to taste.
» Serve immediately with Crunchy Tortilla Chips (page 142), Steak Fajitas (page 53), Chicken Enchiladas (page 110) or other Tex-Mex dishes.

NOTE This should be eaten on the day you make it. It is not much good the next day. You can, however, mix this in with a roasted salsa and it still tastes great and will keep a little better. Adding a dash of vinegar will help it last longer.

* *

TEXAS TOAST

Serves 4

* *

I used to eat this or a variation of this about 4–5 times a week when I was a kid. I taught my wife how to make it. Texas toast is now a mainstay of her diet. This is the only 'dessert' I make. Why would you want to make anything else?

INGREDIENTS

4 slices thick-sliced toasting bread
2 oz (100 g) butter
1 teaspoon garlic powder
2 oz (60 g) cheese, for melting

1 tablespoon scallions (spring onions) or parsley, finely chopped
honey or maple syrup, to taste

METHOD

» Spread butter lightly over toasting bread and put into a frypan (skillet) or directly on a hot, clean barbecue steel plate.
» Cook on each side until lightly browned.
» Place on a baking sheet and sprinkle hot toast lightly with garlic powder. Cover with cheese.
» Place over indirect heat on your barbecue, under the grill (broiler) in your oven at about 400F° (200°C) for 5–7 minutes or until cheese has melted.
» Sprinkle with scallions or parsley then drizzle with honey or maple syrup.
» Serve warm.

NOTE You can serve this with jam or just about anything you like.

* *

BARBECUED DEVILLED EGGS

Serves 6-12

The beginnings of what we call 'devilled eggs' can be traced back to ancient Rome. In the 4th and 5th centuries C.E., eggs were boiled, seasoned and then served at the start of a meal. This was known as a gustatio. In the 13th century, stuffed eggs began to appear in Andalusia, which is now a part of Spain. The first-known printed mention of 'devil' as a culinary term appeared in Great Britain in 1786. And I thought they started in Texas. November 2nd is National Deviled Egg Day in the US, believe it or not.

INGREDIENTS

12 free range eggs

8 fl oz (250 ml) mayonnaise

2 tablespoons apple cider vinegar

½ teaspoon brown sugar

1 tablespoon mustard

3 tablespoons corn relish

2 jalapeños, seeds removed and finely diced

4 slices streaky bacon, dry-fried and crumbled

1½ teaspoons smoky paprika powder

METHOD

» Boil the eggs to soft or medium, about 5–7 minutes.

» Peel eggs and slice them lengthwise down the middle.

» Remove the yolks, put them in a mixing bowl and mash with a fork.

» Add the mayonnaise, vinegar, sugar, mustard and corn relish and combine together well.

» Blend in the jalapeños and bacon.

» Fill each egg with the mixture.

» Sprinkle with paprika and chill.

» Serve as a side or appetizer.

NOTE Throughout history and all around the world, cooks have tried all kinds of variations on the filling—including dill pickles, chopped fresh dill, crab meat, wasabi and caviar among many others. Why don't you try some of these or make up your own devilish mixture?

TEXAS STYLE COLESLAW

Serves 8-10

* *

A must for a Texan-style barbecue—it is best to prepare this the day before you want to serve.

INGREDIENTS

1 medium red cabbage, half chopped and half shredded

1 green cabbage, half chopped and half shredded

1 large white onion, finely diced

2 carrots, peeled and grated

½ red bell pepper (capsicum), diced

½ yellow bell pepper (capsicum), diced

sugar, to taste

½ teaspoon dry mustard

2 tablespoons Italian parsley, finely chopped

1 teaspoon salt

¼ teaspoon freshly ground black pepper

Dressing

2 fl oz (60 ml) extra virgin olive oil

4 fl oz (120 ml) apple cider vinegar

METHOD

» Add cabbage, onions, carrots and bell peppers to a large mixing bowl and mix together.

» Add sugar, mustard and parsley. Season with salt and pepper to taste.

» Mix the dressing ingredients together. Pour the dressing over the coleslaw.

» Place in the refrigerator for 24 hours to allow the flavors to come together.

» Serve with your favorite barbecued meats.

NOTE If you're cutting down on sugar, you can eliminate it all together. Texans like their coleslaw with a bit of sugar, though.

* *

CREAMED RADISHES AND SPINACH

You can make radishes and spinach one of the family favorites. Just cook them like this.

INGREDIENTS

1 bunch spinach, washed and drained
1 bunch large red radishes, washed and drained
1½ tablespoons butter
2 tablespoons flour

8 fl oz (250 ml) milk
salt and freshly ground black pepper, to taste
2 tablespoons cheddar cheese, or more according to
   taste

METHOD

» Wash spinach and radishes.
» Cut the spinach into ribbons. Pare and slice the radishes into circles.
» Boil the spinach and radish in separate saucepans for 1 minute. Pour off excess water and combine them in one pot.
» Melt the butter in another saucepan and whisk in the flour.
» Add milk, salt and pepper, and 1 tablespoon of the cheese and mix.
» Add the radishes and spinach to the sauce. Stir well.
» Serve hot with the rest of the cheese sprinkled on top.

CRISPY SHALLOTS

Serves 4

* *

These are delicious and something you can't stop eating. So don't even try. Serve some of these on your homemade hamburgers.

INGREDIENTS

16 fl oz (500 ml) extra virgin olive oil, for frying
5 scallions (spring onions), thinly sliced
16 fl oz (500 ml) milk
8 oz (250 g) all-purpose (plain) flour

1 tablespoon onion powder
1 tablespoon garlic powder
salt and freshly ground black pepper, to taste

METHOD

» In a skillet or deep fryer, heat the oil to about 350°F (180°C).
» Place the thinly sliced shallots in milk.
» Combine flour, onion and garlic powders together. Coat the milk-covered shallots with the dry mixture.
» Add to the hot oil and cook, stirring until golden brown, about 2 minutes.
» Place the shallots on a paper towel or where they can drain.
» Sprinkle with salt to taste while still warm.
» Allow to rest for 2–3 minutes and serve.

NOTE Ever heard of onion rings? Make them the same way.

* *

My grandfather W. Ed. Murphy, second right

POTATO FANS

Serves 4

* *

Kids love these. Correction—*everyone* loves these. Make extra and serve with bandages as everyone will be fighting over them.

INGREDIENTS

2 slices streaky bacon
5 oz (150 g) extra virgin olive oil
4 medium potatoes, skin on
4 oz (125 g) butter, melted
2 teaspoons salt
½ teaspoon pepper

¼ teaspoon cumin
¼ teaspoon parsley or thyme
5 oz (160 ml) Parmesan cheese, grated
5 oz (160 ml) cheddar cheese, grated
8 oz (250 g) sour cream (optional), to serve

METHOD

» Cook bacon in a frypan lightly greased with 1 oz (30 g) of olive oil until crispy. Cool, crumble and set aside.
» Wash potatoes thoroughly. Slice a thin strip off the bottom of each potato so they sit flat.
» Slice through each potato 15–20 times, but don't slice all the way through. The potato is supposed to fan out from the bottom, so you need the bottom part of the potato to hold the fan.
» Whisk together the butter with the remaining oil in a bowl. Salt and pepper to taste. Drizzle or brush the potato surface with half the butter and oil mix.
» Place potatoes on a greased baking tray and cook for about 30 minutes or until potatoes are cooked through.
» Remove and brush potatoes with the rest of butter and oil. Add the bacon and herbs with the cheese on top.
» Cook until potatoes are crispy and fan out a bit and the cheese has melted on top.
» Serve hot with sour cream if you wish or your favorite accompaniment.

NOTE There are all kinds of things you can add to this recipe–diced sausage, chili, chopped fresh tomatoes, onion, or anything else you can think of.

* *

SPANISH OMELET

Serves 6

* *

This is how you feed a whole bunch of folks for breakfast. Just make this, serve with toast and you're done.

INGREDIENTS

10 large eggs
6 fl oz (200 ml) milk
2 fl oz (60 ml) cream
8 oz (250 g) cheese, grated
butter or cooking oil, for cooking
3 slices streaky bacon, fried crisply and crumbled
1 Kransky sausage (or any breakfast-style sausage),
  fried crisply and diced
1 medium red bell pepper (capsicum), diced
1 small red onion, diced
¼ bunch cilantro (coriander), finely chopped
2 tomatoes, thinly sliced
2 tablespoons oil
salt and freshly ground black pepper to taste

METHOD

» Preheat barbecue or oven to 400°F (200°C).
» Crack the eggs in a large bowl and mix with milk and cream.
» Into a well-buttered or well-oiled cooking tray, pour half the egg mixture and sprinkle with a little of the cheese, then add bacon, Kransky, bell pepper, onion and cilantro. Pour over the rest of the egg mixture and add more cheese (leave a little to sprinkle on top later).
» Place the tomato slices on top and cover with tin foil.
» Cook for about 35 minutes or until the mixture no longer wobbles in the center. Uncover and sprinkle with the remaining cheese. Put under the grill to color and crisp just a little.
» Season to taste.
» Serve with toast.

NOTE You can make sandwiches out of the leftovers as the omelet will last in
the fridge for a couple of days.

* *

CRUNCHY TORTILLA CHIPS

Serves 6

* *

You might never buy another tortilla chip (tostadas) again. This is so easy, you won't believe it. But, it's got to be corn tortillas.

INGREDIENTS

3 packets corn tortillas, 6 inch (15 cm)

8 pt (4 L) cooking oil, for frying

salt, to taste

salsa or dip of choice, to serve

METHOD

» Cut tortillas like a pie into 4 quarters.

» Preheat deep fryer or frypan. Set your temperature at 320º–340ºF (160º–170ºC).

» Drop in quartered corn tortillas.

» Cook for only a few seconds until they start to bubble and turn brown.

» Remove and place on a wire rack or quickly toss on paper towels. Sprinkle with salt while they are still warm.

» Allow to rest for 1–2 minutes.

» Serve warm with a salsa (pages 169–172) or dip of your choice.

NOTE You can keep these for a while. The next day they actually get crispier and crunchier.

* *

BARBECUED RED BEANS

Serves 6

* *

This is a very tasty alternative to opening a can of beans. It's worth it to make your own—they are much better.

INGREDIENTS

16 oz (500 g) borlotti beans or red beans

12 oz (375 g) Beef Stock (page 153)

1 tablespoon tomato paste

15 oz (425 g) tomatoes, diced (or 1 can)

3 fl oz (90 ml) molasses

2 teaspoons extra virgin olive oil

3 slices streaky bacon, chopped

2 cloves garlic, chopped

1 small onion, finely chopped

1 teaspoon mustard seeds

1 teaspoon sweet paprika

1 teaspoon salt

¼ teaspoon freshly ground black pepper

¼ teaspoon dried ground sage

2 fl oz (60 ml) white vinegar

butter or cooking oil, for greasing

METHOD

» Wash the beans and soak for at least one hour in a large Dutch oven-type cooking pot.

» Drain the water from the beans. Replace in the Dutch oven and add the stock, tomato paste, diced tomatoes and molasses.

» Bring to a boil, reduce heat and simmer for about an hour or until beans are tender. Drain and set aside.

» Preheat the barbecue to medium high, 400°F (200°C).

» Heat the oil in a medium skillet on the barbecue.

» Add the bacon, garlic and onion and sauté for a couple of minutes. Remove from heat and mix together with the beans mixture.

» Add mustard seeds, paprika, salt, pepper, sage and vinegar. Stir to combine.

» Transfer to a large, well-oiled or well-buttered baking tray or dish. Cover with foil.

» Barbecue over indirect heat (or in the oven) at about 350–400ºF (175–200º C) until the sauce thickens to coat the beans, about 40 minutes. Check after 20 minutes and stir as required.

» Serve immediately.

NOTE Leftovers can be stored in a sealed container in the refrigerator for up to a week or freeze. You can also cook these with a ham hock for extra flavor.

* *

BLACK-EYED PEA SOUP

Serves 8-10

* *

In the US it is traditional to serve this on New Year's Eve. So start practicing now, in case you find yourself on New Year's Eve without your black-eyed soup.

INGREDIENTS

16 oz (500 g) shelled, black-eyed peas

16 oz (500 g) ham hock

12 fl oz (375 ml) Beef Stock (page 153) or 1 beef
  bouillon cube dissolved in same amount of water

extra virgin olive oil, for cooking

1 medium Spanish or white onion, finely diced

2–3 scallions (spring onions), chopped

2 cloves garlic, crushed

12–15 green beans, cut into 1 inch (2.5 cm) pieces

½ bunch cilantro (coriander), chopped

8 oz (250 g) tomato puree or diced tomatoes

2 tablespoons salt

2 tablespoons black pepper

12 oz (375 g) ham, shredded or diced

2 cheese Kranskys, sliced thinly and fried until
  golden brown

4 slices streaky bacon, crispy fried and crumbled

12 oz (375 g) cherry tomatoes

METHOD

» Sort the black-eyed peas and discard any stones or damaged peas.

» Rinse peas until the water runs clean then place in a large saucepan with water for at least one hour, or soak overnight.

» Drain the peas and add the ham hock. Add stock until the peas are covered and the ham hock is almost covered (add water if necessary). Bring to the boil, then turn the heat to a simmer.

» Add oil to a saucepan and sauté onion, scallion and garlic over gentle heat until onion is translucent.

» Add drained beans, cilantro, tomato puree, salt and pepper. Cover with a lid and simmer for about 1 hour.

» Make sure that the whole mixture is covered. Add extra water or stock if it starts to dry out. After an hour, remove the ham hock, trim off and discard the fat. Cut the meat from the hock into small pieces and return to the pot with the ham hock bone.

» Cook the diced ham in a frypan a little olive oil until crispy. Add the crispy bacon pieces and Kranskys. Remove the ham bones.

» Add cherry tomatoes and keep simmering for another 10 minutes.

» Serve in soup bowls.

NOTE Use this recipe to make Easy Texan Caviar (page 124).

* *

ROASTED SPICY VEGETABLES

Serves 5

* *

This dish would make you want to turn vegetarian. As much as I like to cook and eat meat, this is an alternative that is just as good or better. We all need to eat more fresh vegetables. Make sure you buy them when they are best at their peak.

INGREDIENTS

5 small potatoes

5 baby carrots

5 yellow pumpkin (squash) pieces

2 large red onions, peeled and cut in quarters

3 medium beetroots, cut into quarters

4 tablespoons extra virgin olive oil

2 cloves garlic, crushed

¼ bunch cilantro (coriander), chopped

¼ bunch parsley, (chopped)

1 tablespoon paprika

1 teaspoon cumin

1 teaspoon chili powder, optional

1 tablespoon salt

1 tablespoon pepper

METHOD

» Preheat hooded barbecue or oven to 250ºF (125ºC). Wash and dry all the vegetables. Peal and cut the pumpkin into pieces twice the size of carrots and small potatoes so they all cook at the same rate. Place the vegetables in a large baking tray.

» Drizzle vegetables with half the oil and move them around a bit to make sure all the surfaces are covered. Combine garlic, cilantro, parsley, paprika, cumin, chili (if using), salt and pepper. Sprinkle about half of the spices over the vegetables.

» Put the vegetables onto the barbecue with hood down and cook for about 10 minutes.

» Remove from heat. Drizzle with the remaining oil and sprinkle the rest of the spices over the vegetables.

» Place back in covered barbecue to continue cooking for about 20–25 minutes. At the 20-minute mark, test with a fork to see if vegetables are cooked. Allow a few more minutes if not.

» Serve hot.

* *

WHOLE STUFFED BARBECUED PUMPKIN

Serves 4–6

• •

This is a vegetable made for the barbecue. It is huge, heavy and packed with good stuff. Perfect for serving with turkey legs at your next caveman's party.

INGREDIENTS

2–3 lb (1–1.5 kg) pumpkin
1 oz (30 g) unsalted butter
1 large onion, chopped
8 slices streaky bacon, chopped
1 oz (500 g) breadcrumbs, homemade if you have time
3 cloves garlic, crushed
2 tablespoons sage leaves, chopped (or parsley and/or

cilantro/coriander)
salt and freshly ground black pepper, to taste
8 oz (250 g) Swiss cheese, grated
8 oz (250 g) tasty cheese, shredded
8 fl oz (250 ml) cream
olive oil cooking spray

METHOD

» Preheat the oven or barbecue to 350ºF (180˚C).
» Cut off the top of the pumpkin, but keep it as intact as possible because you'll need it as a lid.
» Remove all seeds and fibrous material from the middle of the pumpkin to create a hollow cavity.
» Melt butter in a frypan over the barbecue grill. Add onion and bacon and sauté for 2–3 minutes.
» Add the breadcrumbs, garlic and sage to the onion and bacon mix. Season well with salt and pepper to taste. Stir in the cheeses and melt them slightly.
» Remove the mixture from the heat and pack the mixture into the hollow of the pumpkin.
» Add the cream into the now-filled pumpkin hollow.
» Replace the pumpkin lid.
» Reduce the barbecue heat to 250–300ºF (120–150ºC).
» Place a foil baking tin on a large baking tray. Inside the foil tin, place several wide sheets of foil large enough to completely cover the pumpkin. Place the pumpkin in the middle of the foil. Lightly spray the pumpkin completely with the oil. Wrap the pumpkin in the foil to enclose it completely.
» Place on the barbecue and bake for 2–3 hours, or until tender. Test to make sure it is cooked by piercing the pumpkin with a skewer. Remove from heat and allow to rest for about 5 minutes.
» Serve hot as a main or as a side dish with any meats, such as a roast or brisket.

NOTE For a Tex-Mex style, throw in some chopped jalapeños (without seeds).

• •

Chapter 5

STOCKS
SAUCES
SALSAS

BEEF STOCK

• •

This is the base for any of your beef or pork dishes that need liquid. Use this instead of water to get a depth of flavor into all of your dishes. I like to eat fresh vegetables and I don't cook them if they are not at their peak. However, for making stock, 'off-peak' vegetables are still good to use.

INGREDIENTS

5 marrow bones, cut into 1 inch (2.5 cm) sections
16 fl oz (500 ml) boiling water
1 beef stock cube
½ bunch celery
5 medium carrots

3 large brown onions
1 head red or green cabbage
5 cloves garlic, chopped
1 tablespoon salt
1 tablespoon pepper

METHOD

» In a large, deep saucepan or Dutch oven, add the olive oil and begin to heat.

» Place the marrow bones in the hot oil and cook for about 2 minutes.

» Dissolve the stock cube in boiling water and add to the marrow bones.

» Roughly cut the celery, carrots, onion and cabbage. Add to the stock with garlic, salt and pepper.

» Heat to bring to the boil, then cover and turn to simmer over a very low heat for at least 3 hours or more. It can go all day or all night because slow and steady wins this race. Top up with water every few hours.

» The stock is sufficiently cooked when the meat and marrow fall off the bones.

» Remove from heat and when cooled slightly, strain the contents.

» Discard the bones and vegetables. If you like, you can add the strained vegetables to the Texas Cowboy Barbecue Sauce (page 154).

• •

STOCKS SAUCES SALSAS

QUICK BARBECUE SAUCE

* *

If you're in a hurry and you need some barbecue sauce (pictured left) on short notice, try this.

INGREDIENTS

8 fl oz (250 ml) honey or maple syrup

8 fl oz (250 ml) ketchup

2 fl oz (60 ml) lemon juice

1 tablespoon Worcestershire sauce

1 tablespoon soy sauce

1 clove garlic, minced

1 teaspoon Tabasco sauce

½ teaspoon salt

½ teaspoon pepper

METHOD

» Combine all ingredients in a saucepan. Bring to the boil, then turn to simmer and stir well. Reduce until it reaches the desired consistency.

GREEN BARBECUE SAUCE

* *

This sauce is an ideal accompaniment for barbecued chicken, fish or shrimp (prawns). Tomatillos, also known as husk tomatoes, are originally from Mexico. They are green or green-purple in color, small and round in size and have a tart flavor.

INGREDIENTS

8 oz (250 g) green tomatoes, coarsely chopped

10 tomatillos, husked and coarsely chopped

2 cloves garlic, diced

3 oz (100 g) sugar

4 fl oz (125 ml) white vinegar

1 large onion, coarsely chopped

1 tablespoon dry mustard, ground

½ teaspoon dried red pepper (chili) powder

1 teaspoon salt

METHOD

» Place all the ingredients in a non-reactive saucepan and cook over a medium-low heat for about 1 hour, or until tomatoes and tomatillos are tender.

» Cool and blend the mixture in batches in a food processor until smooth.

» Serve with your favorite barbecued chicken, fish or shrimp.

NOTE If you can't get your hands on tomatillos, just use double the quantity of green tomatoes. Store any leftovers in a sealed glass container for up to 3 days.

* *

BLACK BUTTER SAUCE

* *

INGREDIENTS

1 oz (30 g) butter

2 cloves garlic, sliced thinly

1 oz (30 g) balsamic vinegar

1 jalapeño, finely diced

2 tablespoons tomato paste

1 tablespoon freshly ground black pepper

½ tablespoon chili flakes

½ tablespoon salt

1 teaspoon dry ground mustard

METHOD

» Melt the butter in a saucepan then add garlic and vinegar. Simmer over a low heat to make sure that the sauce doesn't burn.

» Reduce until you have a third of the original quantity. Add the remaining ingredients and use immediately.

NOTE This sauce is used for the Steak and Lobster Sliders (page 62). It goes well with meat and seafood alike.

CHEESY HORSERADISH CREAM SAUCE

* *

This homemade horseradish cream really adds to the flavors of a barbecued prime rib, or any other steak for that matter.

INGREDIENTS

16 oz (500 g) cheddar cheese, finely grated

4 oz (125 g) plain Greek yogurt

1 tablespoon prepared horseradish

½ teaspoon salt

freshly ground black pepper

METHOD

» Combine all the ingredients.

» Chill until ready to serve.

NOTE This recipe uses store-bought horseradish. If you want to use fresh horseradish root, peel and chop and whiz in a blender with a little vinegar, salt and enough water to make a paste.

* *

CHICKEN WINGS HOT SAUCE

* *

This hot sauce goes well with chicken wings, naturally.

INGREDIENTS

2 tablespoons butter

4 oz (125 g) Tabasco sauce

3 tablespoons honey

3 teaspoons garlic powder

3 tablespoons soy sauce

METHOD

» Melt butter in a frypan. Add hot sauce, honey, garlic powder and soy. Simmer for about 15 minutes and serve (with chicken wings).

CHIMICHURRI SAUCE

* *

Chimichurri is a green sauce, originally from Argentina, which is delicious with any grilled meat, served on grilled vegetables or on pasta. It can also be used as a marinade, basting sauce or even as a dipping sauce.

INGREDIENTS

8 oz (250 g) Italian parsley, chopped

4 tablespoons cilantro (coriander), chopped

2 teaspoons red chili flakes

4 fl oz (125 ml) extra virgin olive oil

1 tablespoon balsamic vinegar

3 cloves garlic, minced or crushed

¾ teaspoon coarse sea salt

½ teaspoon freshly ground black pepper

METHOD

» Combine all the ingredients and chill in the refrigerator.

» Remove from refrigerator to serve at room temperature.

* *

TEXAS COWBOY BARBECUE SAUCE

* *

If you want a real challenge, go ahead and give this a try. You'd better have a big pot for this one. This barbecue sauce goes well with just about anything—except fruit, maybe. If you have a huge barbecue, a huge number of friends to feed and you need a huge amount of sauce, this is for you.

INGREDIENTS

2 pt (1 L) Beef Stock (page 153)

4 pt (2 L) passata (store-bought) or tomato puree

4 fl oz (125 ml) tamari or soy sauce

24 oz (750 g) diced tomatoes

½ bunch celery, roughly chopped

3 medium onions, rough chopped and roasted

5 medium carrots, roughly chopped and roasted

3 jalapeños, seeds removed and roasted

6 fl oz (180 ml) Worcestershire sauce (Lea & Perrin for wheat-free)

6 fl oz (180 ml) golden syrup (or molasses/rice syrup)

6 fl oz (180 ml) apple cider vinegar

3 lemons, juiced and seeds removed

½ bunch cilantro (coriander), chopped

2 tablespoons paprika

1 tablespoon cayenne pepper

1 tablespoon celery salt

2 tablespoons mustard powder

2 tablespoons cumin powder

2 tablespoons garlic powder

1 tablespoon chili powder

1 tablespoon onion powder

1 tablespoon freshly ground black pepper

juice of 2 oranges, freshly squeezed, to taste

METHOD

» Add the beef stock to a very large, deep cooking pot. Turn the heat on to medium-high.

» Pour in the passata, tamari and the diced tomatoes. Add the celery, roasted onions, carrots and jalapeños. Bring to a boil and turn back the heat to simmer.

» Add Worcestershire sauce, golden syrup, vinegar, lemon juice, cilantro, paprika, cayenne pepper, celery salt, spice powders, salt and pepper.

» Bring back to the boil then turn the heat back to simmer.

» Cover and simmer for 2–3 hours, stirring at least every 15 minutes.

» Taste for sweetness, if it is not sweet enough add orange juice and taste—when you can taste a hint of sweetness do not add any more.

» Remove from heat and allow to cool. Strain and retain the liquid in a large bowl (or another large pot).

» Blend the strained vegetables until smooth. Pour the blended vegetables back into the sauce and stir well.

» Return the saucepan to the heat. Bring back to the boil then cover and reduce heat to simmer for a further 15–20 minutes.

» Taste regularly and adjust by adding salt, pepper or ketchup to thicken and add sweetness. Adjust according to taste. You can make it hotter by adding extra chili powder.

» Remove the lid and continue to simmer for a few hours to reduce the sauce to the desired consistency.

* *

RED WINE MUSTARD SAUCE

INGREDIENTS

2–3 tablespoons extra virgin olive oil

1 medium white onion, chopped

2 stalks celery, finely chopped

2 fl oz (60 ml) liquid cane sugar

8 fl oz (250 ml) ketchup

4 fl oz (125 ml) Beef Stock (page 153)

2 tablespoons red wine vinegar

2 teaspoons dry mustard

½ teaspoon cayenne pepper

½ teaspoon salt

1 teaspoon vegetable oil

½ teaspoon lemon juice

METHOD

» Add the olive oil to a cast iron frypan (skillet) and place on direct heat on the barbecue grill. Add the chopped onion and sauté. Stir in the other ingredients and mix together.

» Bring to a boil, then simmer and reduce. Set aside until ready to use.

NOTE This sauce is used for the Barbecued Pork Chops (page 75) but goes well with any barbecued meats.

HONEY MUSTARD SAUCE

INGREDIENTS

4 fl oz (120 ml) honey

4 fl oz (120 ml) Dijon mustard

2 tablespoons fresh herbs of choice, chopped

METHOD

» Combine all ingredients thoroughly in a bowl.

» Cover and keep in the refrigerator.

NOTE This will keep in an air-tight container in the refrigerator for a day. Use maple syrup instead of honey, if you prefer.

HONEY MANGO BARBECUE SAUCE

This goes well with pulled pork, steaks or fried chicken. I really like this as a pizza base and it's great as a marinade too.

INGREDIENTS

2 teaspoons extra virgin olive oil

4 fl oz (125 ml) honey

2 fl oz (60 ml) maple syrup

2 cloves garlic, crushed

½ red pepper (chili) flakes (optional)

½ teaspoon salt

pinch of ground cloves

2 teaspoons Dijon mustard

8 fl oz (250 ml) tomato sauce, store bought can

1 mango, peeled and puréed or 8 fl oz (250 ml) mango juice

METHOD

» Preheat a heavy-based cast iron skillet, or equivalent frypan, over a medium heat.

» Remove the skillet and turn off the heat—from this point you'll need to work quickly as you'll only be using the retained heat in the skillet to start off.

» Add the light extra virgin olive oil to the skillet.

» Add the vinegar, honey, maple syrup, garlic, salt, red pepper flakes, ground cloves, Dijon mustard, chili powder and cayenne pepper to the pan and mix well.

» Turn the stove-top back on and now heat the mixture over medium-high heat until it boils. Reduce to low and allow to simmer for 2–3 minutes.

» Add the tomato sauce and mango puree and mix in well. Let simmer for a further 5 minutes. Remove from heat and allow to cool.

» Serve immediately as a side to your favorite barbecue recipes.

NOTE This sauce won't last very long, but you can prolong its life in the refrigerator if you add a little vinegar. Store in an airtight container for 3–4 days or freeze.

Tomahawk steak, see page 49.

HORSERADISH MUSTARD SAUCE

This goes especially well with roast beef and can also double as a dip.

INGREDIENTS

1 tablespoon prepared horseradish
1 tablespoon Dijon mustard
2 fl oz (60 ml) buttermilk
1 tablespoon sour cream

1 teaspoon freshly ground black pepper
½ teaspoon salt
½ teaspoon rosemary, chopped finely

METHOD

» Mix all ingredients in small bowl and lightly whip to blend.
» Cover and chill in the refrigerator until use.

NOTE This sauce can be made a day ahead, but won't keep for longer
than that, so it's best made fresh.

ROASTED SALSA

This is the number one dip in South America. Salsa simply means 'sauce', and in English-speaking countries, this term usually refers to the sauces typical of Mexican cuisine. Known as *salsa picante*, they are often tomato based and spicy from mild to extremely hot—and they make great dips.

INGREDIENTS

8–10 whole tomatoes (or cooking tomatoes)

4 medium jalapeño peppers, halved and with seeds removed

3 medium white onions, cut into eight pieces

4 large cloves garlic

1 tablespoon salt

1 teaspoon freshly ground black pepper

½ bunch cilantro (coriander)

½–1 lime, juiced, to taste

salt and freshly ground black pepper, to taste

Crunchy Tortilla Chips (page 142), to serve

METHOD

» Preheat barbecue plate or oven to moderate, 350°F (180°C).

» Place the tomatoes, jalapeños, onions and 3 garlic cloves directly on the barbecue plate. Cook until they start to burn at the edges and they become soft.

» Remove from heat. Skin the tomatoes and remove the core. Add to a blender with the jalapeños, onion and garlic and pulse until they have a rough, slightly-diced appearance. Add cilantro to the mix and blend very slightly.

» Add the lime juice, the remaining garlic clove (chopped), and salt and pepper. Blend quickly again but don't mix it too smoothly.

» Now put the rough-blended mixture into a saucepan and heat.

» Add more salt or pepper to taste.

» Serve warm or cold with Crunchy Tortilla Chips.

NOTE Salsa is best served as fresh as possible. It never lasts long anyway. If you want to keep your salsa for a day or two, add some vinegar, lime juice and/or crushed garlic before storing. A study on salsa food hygiene described refrigeration as 'the key' to safe sauces. The fresh lime juice and/or fresh garlic helps prevent the growth of bacteria.

AVOCADO AND PINEAPPLE SALSA

* *

This salsa is delicious—sweet, spicy and a little tangy.

INGREDIENTS

1 clove garlic, finely chopped

2 tablespoons orange juice, freshly squeezed

1 tablespoon lime juice, freshly squeezed

1 teaspoon orange zest

½ teaspoon honey

1 tablespoon extra virgin olive oil

½ teaspoon salt

½ teaspoon freshly ground black pepper

1 large pineapple, peeled, core removed, cut into ½ inch (1 cm) pieces

1 avocado

METHOD

» Combine all the ingredients except the avocado in a bowl.

» Just before serving, peel the avocado and cut into ½ inch (1 cm) pieces. Be gentle when mixing the avocado pieces into the salsa so that they retain their shape.

» Serve with your favorite barbecue recipe.

NOTE If you don't like pineapple, leave it out and just have an avocado salsa. Avocado salsa goes really well with chicken wraps and potato wedges served with a dollop of sour cream.

BLACKBERRY SALSA

* *

This is a tangy, sweet salsa that adds flavor and color. Bonus—it's also very quick and easy to make.

INGREDIENTS

8 oz (250 g) ripe blackberries (frozen and thawed will do at a pinch)

3 tablespoons red onion, minced

1 clove garlic, minced

1 jalapeño, finely diced, seeds removed

2 tablespoons cilantro (coriander) leaves, finely chopped

1 teaspoon lime juice

1 tablespoon honey

½ teaspoon salt

METHOD

» Combine all ingredients and mix well.

» Place in the refrigerator in an airtight container.

» Serve slightly chilled.

* *

MANGO SALSA

This salsa goes well with any barbecued chicken, vegetables or fish. It is also delicious with fajitas, chips or with avocado.

INGREDIENTS

4 oz (125 g) tomatoes, diced
4 oz (125 g) firm, slightly green mango, diced
2 tablespoons cilantro (coriander), diced
1 scallion (spring onion), diced, stems and all

1 tablespoon honey
2 tablespoons lime juice, freshly squeezed
3 tablespoons plain, unsweetened yogurt

METHOD

» Combine the tomatoes, mango, cilantro and scallion in a bowl.
» Use a smaller bowl to combine the honey, lime juice and yogurt then mix the mango mixture with the yogurt mixture.
» Keep in the refrigerator and serve slightly chilled.

PEACH SALSA

This is the perfect salsa to serve with crunchy tortilla chips or as a topping for tacos, tortilla chips or even grilled meats, chicken or vegetables.

INGREDIENTS

2 large firm peaches
½ small red onion, finely diced
2 limes, freshly juiced
1 jalapeño, diced, seeds removed

2 tablespoons mint
2 tablespoons cilantro (coriander)
1 teaspoon salt
¼ teaspoon freshly ground black pepper

METHOD

» Wash and dice the peaches into ½ inch (1 cm) pieces. Combine in a bowl with all the other ingredients.
» Keep in the refrigerator in an airtight container.
» Serve slightly chilled.

NOTE You can use canned peaches as an alternative if peaches are out of season.

WATERMELON SALSA

The watermelon provides the crush in this sweet, savory salsa that is the perfect accompaniment for grilled pork or chicken. It also goes well with ribs or you can try it with Crunchy Tortilla Chips (page 142) as a change from tomato salsa.

INGREDIENTS

2 lb (1 kg) seedless watermelon, diced
1 small red onion, diced
4 oz (125 g) chopped cilantro (coriander)
1 jalapeño, diced, seeds removed
⅓ yellow bell pepper (capsicum), diced

1 teaspoon mint, chopped
1 lime, freshly juiced
½ teaspoon salt
½ teaspoon pepper

METHOD

» Place watermelon, onion, cilantro, jalapeño, bell pepper and mint into a bowl and mix together.
» Add lime juice and season with salt and pepper to taste.
» Chill slightly in refrigerator and serve.

TEXAN WHITE GRAVY

Not technically a sauce, this is the standard Texan way of making gravy from juices that are left in a baking dish or frypan after cooking meat, especially chicken. It is the traditional companion of Texas Biscuits—in other parts of the world, these would be called 'scones'.

INGREDIENTS

pan juices
2 tablespoons all-purpose (plain) flour

salt and freshly ground black pepper, to taste
8 fl oz (250 ml) milk

METHOD

» Pour off most of the fat on top of the pan juices (or spoon off) leaving about 1½–2 tablespoons of juice.
» Sprinkle flour all over the pan. Whisk or stir with a fork. Heat to combine juices and flour. Season with salt and black pepper.
» Pour in the milk, gradually, a little at a time, into the pan stirring constantly. Add more milk if the gravy gets too thick.
» Bring to a boil, then simmer and stir until you get the consistency you like.

MURPHY'S RANCH DRESSING

This goes well with steak fingers, chicken ribs, potato chips and French fries. It makes a great dip as well.

INGREDIENTS

1 teaspoons paprika

1 teaspoons salt

1 teaspoons sugar

1 teaspoon pepper

1 teaspoon garlic powder

12 fl oz (375 ml) sour cream

6 fl oz (180 ml) yogurt

6 fl oz (180 ml) mayonnaise

4 medium scallions (spring onions), chopped finely

pinch of saffron

METHOD

» Combine the dry ingredients in a bowl, except for the saffron.

» Add sour cream, yogurt, mayonnaise, scallions and saffron.

» Mix thoroughly.

» Cool in the refrigerator for 1–2 hours before pouring over your favorite salad leaves.

NOTE This dressing will keep in the refrigerator for up to 3 days.

HONEY MUSTARD LIME DRESSING

This is a wonderfully tangy dressing for green salads.

INGREDIENTS

2 tablespoons mayonnaise

2 tablespoons Dijon mustard,

1 tablespoon lime juice

2 tablespoons honey

2 tablespoons rice wine vinegar

1 clove garlic, finely minced

¼ teaspoon onion powder

¼ teaspoon salt

1 teaspoon Worcestershire Sauce

1 jalapeño, diced (no seeds)

2 tablespoons extra virgin olive oil

METHOD

» Add all ingredients except oil to a blender or food processor and blend until well combined. Add the oil and continue to blend until a creamy consistency.

» Chill, preferably overnight before using.

Chapter 6

MARINADES

BEEF FILET MARINADE

* *

A versatile marinade for any lean cut of beef or venison.

INGREDIENTS

2 medium white onions, finely diced

4 cloves of garlic, minced

6 tablespoons extra virgin olive oil

4 tablespoons chopped parsley

4 tablespoons chopped cilantro (coriander)

2 tablespoons salt

1 tablespoon pepper

METHOD

» Mix all the ingredients together either by hand or in a blender until thoroughly mixed.

» Place marinade in a sealable plastic bag large enough to hold the meat you are using. Squeeze out all the air and marinate for at least 30 minutes to 1 hour or up to 24 hours.

NOTE This marinade should always be made fresh and used immediately.

DR PEPPER MARINADE

* *

This marinade works equally well with beef or pork.

INGREDIENTS

1 can Dr Pepper

½ pt (250 ml) soy sauce

2 oranges, juiced

METHOD

» Combine all ingredients together.

» Use immediately.

* *

FAJITAS MARINADE

* *

Works well on any thin-cut beef, like a flank steak, round steak or minute steak.

INGREDIENTS

3 fresh jalapeño peppers, stems and seeds removed

2 medium onions, yellow or white, chopped

4 tablespoons fresh cilantro (coriander)

6 fl oz (200 ml) Texas Cowboy Barbecue Sauce (page 161) or store-bought sauce without too much sugar.

4 fl oz (125 ml) soy sauce or tamari

2 limes, juiced

1 tablespoon Worcestershire sauce

1½ teaspoons garlic powder

1 teaspoon salt

½ teaspoon ground cumin

METHOD

» Put all ingredients in a blender and blend until smooth. Place marinade in a sealable plastic bag with the meat. Marinate for *at least* 30 minutes to 1 hour or up to 24 hours.

NOTE You can substitute freshly squeezed orange juice for a sweeter result.

SIRLOIN MARINADE

* *

If you just have to marinate that special steak, here is an Asian-Western fusion marinade that works well.

INGREDIENTS

2 tablespoons soy sauce

1 tablespoon extra virgin olive oil

1 tablespoon horseradish

1 tablespoon Worcestershire sauce

½ teaspoon garlic, crushed

½ teaspoon salt

½ teaspoon freshly ground black pepper

METHOD

» Mix all the ingredients together either by hand or in a blender until thoroughly mixed.

» Place the marinade and meat in a sealable plastic bag. Squeeze out all the air.

» Marinate for at least 1–2 hours or up to 24 hours.

* *

STICKY WINGS CHICKEN MARINADE

This marinade was specifically devised for chicken wings. It's not really good for much else but it's very good for its intended purpose.

INGREDIENTS
2 fl oz (60 ml) ketchup
4 fl oz (125 ml) barbecue sauce of choice
2 teaspoons Worcestershire sauce

2 oz (60 ml) brown sugar
2 teaspoons smoked paprika
salt and pepper

METHOD
» In a mixing bowl, add the ketchup, barbecue sauce, Worcestershire sauce, sugar and paprika in a jug. Season with salt and pepper.
» Place chicken wings in a large, shallow ceramic dish. Pour marinade over and turn chicken wings to coat thoroughly. Cover and refrigerate, turning occasionally, for at least 2 hours.

NOTE You might need to add some water to this if it's too thick. A marinade is supposed to penetrate and it can do this more easily if it's more fluid.

LAMB MARINADE

* *

This is a distinctively sweet marinade.

INGREDIENTS

¼ bunch fresh Italian parsley
1 oz (30 g) fresh mint leaves
1 sprig fresh rosemary leaves, finely chopped
2 cloves garlic

1 small red chili, deseeded
2 fl oz (60 ml) lemon juice
3 tablespoons honey
2 tablespoons extra virgin olive oil

METHOD

» Place all ingredients in a food processor and blend until smooth.
» Pour over the lamb, place in a sealable plastic bag and marinate overnight.

RACK OF LAMB MARINADE

* *

This goes well with any lamb meat.

INGREDIENTS

4 cloves garlic, crushed
4 oz (125 g) fresh mint, roughly chopped
2 teaspoons lemon zest, finely grated
2 lemons, juiced
4 fl oz (125 ml) apple cider vinegar
½ pt (250 ml) Beef Stock (page 153)
1 pt (500 ml) tomato passata
1 tablespoon Worcestershire sauce
4 oz (125 g) extra virgin olive oil

1 tablespoon smoked paprika
½ teaspoon cayenne pepper
1 teaspoon ground cilantro (coriander)
1 teaspoon ground cumin
1 tablespoon chili flakes
1 pinch freshly ground black pepper
1 teaspoon salt
½ teaspoon pepper

METHOD

» Place all the ingredients in a blender and mix thoroughly to a smooth consistency.

NOTE The finer the blend, the better. Make this fresh, because this marinade will only keep a couple of days in the refrigerator.

* *

PORK LOIN MARINADE

* *

This marinade is used in Crispy Smoked Pork Loin Chops (page 82) but it goes well with any cut of pork.

INGREDIENTS

3 cloves garlic, minced

3 inch (7.5 cm) piece fresh ginger, finely chopped

2 tablespoons soy sauce

2 tablespoons tomato purée

1 tablespoon Worcestershire sauce

1 tablespoon red wine vinegar

4 tablespoons brown sugar

2 tablespoons lemon juice

1 teaspoon extra virgin olive oil

METHOD

» Place all ingredients in a blender and blend until smooth.

» Put marinade in a sealable plastic bag with the pork loin (or other pork meat). Squeeze out all the air and refrigerate overnight.

CHICKEN BREAST MARINADE

* *

This is enough for 10–15 chicken breasts.

INGREDIENTS

1 large can pineapple juice (about 1½ pints or 750 ml)

½ pint (250 ml) light soy sauce or tamari

6 fl oz (200 ml) cane sugar syrup

1 teaspoon garlic powder

1 teaspoon onion powder

1 teaspoon coarse ground black pepper

METHOD

» Combine all ingredients.

» Prepare fresh as this will not keep for more than a day or two.

* *

Chapter 7

RUBS

BEEF RIB RUB

* *

INGREDIENTS

1 tablespoon garlic powder

1 tablespoon onion powder

1 tablespoon smoked paprika

2 tablespoons brown sugar

1 teaspoon chili powder

1 teaspoon salt

2 teaspoons oregano

mustard of choice or ketchup to lightly coat the ribs

METHOD

» Combine all the ingredients, except for the mustard or ketchup. Prepare fresh as this will not keep for more than a day or two.

» When using this rub, apply mustard or ketchup to the meat first to act as a binder for the rub, then use the rub.

NOTE This rub is for store-purchased ribs not for the custom-cut Dr Pepper Ribs (page 46).

BRISKET RUB

* *

Generally, I just use salt and pepper on my brisket, but if you *want* to use a rub, use this one. This is also an excellent rub for any large cut of beef.

INGREDIENTS

4 oz (125 g) paprika

2 oz (60 g) salt

2 oz (60 g) cane sugar

2 oz (60 g) brown sugar

2 oz (60 g) cumin

2 oz (60 g) chili powder

2 oz (60 g) freshly ground black pepper

2 tablespoons cayenne pepper

METHOD

» Combine all the ingredients.

» Keep in an airtight container for no more than a day or two.

PRIME RIB RUB

* *

INGREDIENTS

8 tablespoons salt

8 fl oz (250 ml) freshly ground black pepper

2 tablespoons flour

2 tablespoons garlic powder

2 tablespoons onion powder

1 tablespoon oregano

METHOD

» Combine all the ingredients. If necessary, when rubbing into the meat, add some oil to help it stick better to the surface.

NOTE Once you cook a bone-in prime rib, you can debone it, rub some more of this rub on the surface and into the areas that you just removed the bone from, put the rib back on the heat and let it cook for a few minutes longer, just to give it a little extra flavor and a nice crust.

TEXAN STEAK RUB

* *

Here is another excellent steak rub that works with most cuts.

INGREDIENTS

2 tablespoons kosher salt

2 teaspoons brown sugar

¼ teaspoon cornstarch

¼ teaspoon garlic powder

¼ teaspoon garlic salt

¼ teaspoon onion powder

½ teaspoon onion salt

½ teaspoon sage

½ teaspoon turmeric

½ teaspoon paprika

½ teaspoon chili powder

1 teaspoon black pepper

METHOD

» Combine all the ingredients.

» Keep in an airtight container for no more than a day or two.

* *

EASY LAMB RUB

* *

As the name implies, this is an easy rub to use when you're short of ingredients or time.

INGREDIENTS

1½ teaspoons onion salt

1½ teaspoons lemon pepper

1½ teaspoons garlic salt

1 teaspoon salt

1 teaspoon brown sugar

METHOD

» Combine all the ingredients.

» Keep in an airtight container for a day or two.

LAMB RUB

* *

This is a good general rub for lamb. It goes particularly well with lamb ribs.

INGREDIENTS

½ teaspoon salt

3 tablespoons freshly ground black pepper

2 tablespoons ground fennel seed

1 tablespoon ground cumin

1 teaspoon ground cinnamon

3 tablespoons chili powder

2 tablespoons dried oregano

1 tablespoon brown sugar

1 tablespoon sugar

METHOD

» Combine all the ingredients.

» Prepare fresh as this will not keep for more than a day or two.

* *

BASIC PORK RIB RUB

* *

This is a really easy rub to make but it is still highly effective and flavorful.

INGREDIENTS

2 tablespoons paprika

2 tablespoons chili powder

2 tablespoons brown sugar

1 tablespoon freshly ground black pepper

1 tablespoon salt

METHOD

» Combine all the ingredients.

» Keep in an airtight container for a day or two.

PORK RIB DRY RUB

* *

If you don't want to marinate your ribs, try this rub instead.

INGREDIENTS

½ cup golden brown sugar, packed

2 oz (60 g) salt

2 oz (60 g) freshly ground black pepper

2 tablespoons ground mustard

2 tablespoons ground cumin

1 tablespoon garlic powder

1 tablespoon onion powder

1 tablespoon paprika

½ teaspoon sage

1 teaspoon ground cayenne pepper

½ teaspoon chili powder

METHOD

» Combine all the ingredients.

» Keep in an airtight container for no more than a day or two.

NOTE The key to an effective rib rub is to remove the layer of silverskin on the inside of the ribs.
Silverskin is not very porous, extremely resistant to cooking and acts as a barrier,
so get that silverskin off.

* *

PORK SHOULDER RUB

* *

This is for 'low and slow' cooking and it works really well as a pre-smoking rub.

INGREDIENTS

1 tablespoon smoked paprika
2 teaspoons brown sugar
1½ teaspoons cayenne pepper
½ teaspoon celery salt
½ teaspoon garlic salt

½ teaspoon dry mustard
½ teaspoon ground black pepper
½ teaspoon onion powder
¼ teaspoon salt

METHOD

» Combine all the ingredients.
» Prepare fresh as this will not keep for more than a day or two.

NOTE Remember that if you're rubbing pork with the skin on, it's a good idea to score the skin and really get in good because the skin acts like a barrier—it isn't very porous and does not accept additional flavors well. The fat barrier also prevents easy absorption, so don't be shy about going in hard.

BARBECUE CHICKEN RUB

* *

Try this as a starter rub on any chicken that you're barbecuing.

INGREDIENTS

1 tablespoon salt
1 tablespoon pepper
1 teaspoon sage
1 teaspoon paprika

1 teaspoon onion powder
1 teaspoon garlic powder
1 bay leaf, crushed

METHOD

» Combine all the ingredients.
» Keep in an airtight container for no more than a day or two.

* *

CHICKEN RUB

* *

Try this on any chicken that you're grilling or baking.

INGREDIENTS

4 oz (125 g) chili powder

4 oz (125 g) brown sugar

4 oz (125 g) salt

4 oz (125 g) fresh ground pepper

2 oz (60 g) dry mustard

2 oz (60 g) ground cumin

ground red pepper (chili), to taste

METHOD

» Combine all the ingredients.

» Prepare fresh as this will not keep for more than a day or two.

NOTE Remember that if you're rubbing chicken, it's a good idea to either remove the skin or put the rub under the skin because the skin itself acts like a barrier—it isn't very porous and does not accept additional flavors well.

* *

GLOSSARY

Barbecue pit does not refer to a pit or hole in the ground for cooking. It's a generic term for steel barbecues.

Bell peppers = Capsicum

Biscuits are "Texan speak" for what are many call 'scones' in other parts of the English-speaking world.

Black-eyed peas = black-eyed beans.

Breast halves = In the US, when we talk about chicken breasts, we mean the whole breast on both sides of the bone. In other countries only what we call a 'breast half' is called a breast.

Broiler = Grill = Salamander—where the heat is coming from the top.

Chicken-fried is an expression for describing a cooking technique where meat is coated in a seasoned flour mixture before frying.

Cilantro = green, fresh leaf coriander—not to be confused with coriander seed.

Crackers = Ritz Crackers = Salad Biscuits = Saltines = Sayo Biscuits = Water Crackers. Even though all these crackers are slightly different, they're similar enough to be interchangeable in many cases, depending on your personal preference.

Direct heat is cooking straight over the top of the heat source: coals, embers, flame or gas flame.

Dutch oven is a cast-iron pot with a lid.

Entrée—in some parts of the world, like in some parts of the USA, 'entrée' does not mean an appetizer but refers to a main course. However, as Texan as I am, in this particular book when I say 'entrée', I mean an appetizer—the first small course of a meal.

Scallions = spring onions = green onions. Varieties of these types of onions vary in different parts of the world and all have different intensities of flavors. Feel free to use what works for you.

Ground = minced.

High heat as defined in this book, means a temperature of around 450°F (230°C) but sometimes higher.

Indirect heat is cooking away from the heat source on a part of an oven or barbecue that is still hot.

Ketchup or Catsup is known in some parts of the world as tomato sauce (see also Tomato sauce). The confusion comes from the way the English language is used differently depending on where you live.

Low heat as defined in this book, means any temperature above 150°F (65°C) but below 225°F (100°C). It's in this range that you typically smoke stuff.

Medium heat as defined in this book, means a temperature over 225°F (100°C) but below 300°F (150°C).

Medium high heat as defined in this book, means a temperature over 300°F (150°C) and up to around 400°F (200°C). If I'm cooking on a grill, I want to start at this temperature.

Oven broiler = Oven grill.

Plow disc or a **Texan wok** is actually really a modified plow disc with horseshoe handles. The center holes of the former plow disc are welded over and the result serves as a large cooking surface that works particularly well for fajitas.

Re-fried beans are red borlotti beans that have been cooked twice. Boiled first in a saucepan for about 3 hours, then mashed and fried. If you can't be bothered, buy them in a can.

Red onion = Spanish Onion.

Reverse sear is a meat cooking technique where you first cook the meat as a long, slow cook, then finish with a high, direct heat has been slow cooked.

Rib-eye = Scotch steak but rib-eye is usually the same piece of meat with the bone left in.

Rotel = Roma tomatoes = Cooking tomatoes.

Scones—see Biscuits.

Silverskin is a thin membrane that acts as an inside lining of ribs. It is non-7

porous and needs to be removed so that flavors from a marinade or rub can penetrate the meat. You can usually remove it by gripping it with a paper towel and peeling or pulling it off.

Steak main is a term referring to situations where steak is the 'hero' or main part of a dish.

Tamari is a light, wheat-free soy sauce that's great if you want to stay gluten-free.

Tapatío sauce is a hot sauce with a specific type of red pepper (tapatío) and garlic base.

Tomato sauce as defined in this book, refers to tomato purée, but see also Ketchup.

Unrendered fat is fat that has not been sufficiently cooked—nicely melted with a hard, caramelized crust on the outside.

INDEX

ACKNOWLEDGEMENTS

Thank you to Nicola Read for your excellent photography, Xavier Waterkeyn for your support during the photoshoot of this book and Southlands Shopping Centre Penrith for providing the food for our recipes.

Thanks to my family in Texas: to my parents—you helped make me strong; to my wife and children whom I love and admire—you are all my very best friends; and to my wife's family for letting me cook Texan food for them for all these years.

To my sister, Maxine, for inspiration—you taught me to have courage, to be positive no matter what, and to make having fun, one of life's essentials.

Thanks to all the people I have worked for, my students and workmates past and present and to the wonderful people who have shaped my life and helped me through.

Thank the Lord for blessing me through the good and bad.

ABOUT THE AUTHOR

Robert Louis Murphy was raised in Breckenridge Texas and spent his youth hunting, fishing, and cooking his own food in the outdoors.

After attending university in Texas, he found himself back in the outdoors working as a cattle rancher, horse trainer, and oilfield worker. He's been a pilot and a professional guide leading hunting tours through Texas.

His survival skills rival Bear Grylls: Robert spent considerable time hunting and shooting for the Texas Wild Game Co-operative. His love of the outdoors is boundless.

As a change from his outdoors' lifestyle, in 2015, Robert and his daughter Lynzey, stole the spotlight on the hit TV series, My Kitchen Rules. The show gave him the opportunity to share his brand of Texan cooking with a wider audience.

Self taught in the art of cooking, Robert is passionate about sharing his love of outdoor cooking, his recipes from his childhood—a Tex-Mex mix that is becoming increasingly popular around the world—and his enthusiasm for the barbecue in this, his first international cookbook, Texan BBQ.